PAY
YOURSELF
WHAT YOU'RE
WORTH

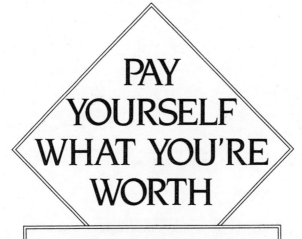

PAY YOURSELF WHAT YOU'RE WORTH

How to Make Terrific Money in Direct Sales

SHIRLEY HUTTON

WITH

CONSTANCE deSWAAN

BANTAM BOOKS

TORONTO • NEW YORK • LONDON • SYDNEY • AUCKLAND

PAY YOURSELF WHAT YOU'RE WORTH
A Bantam Book / March 1988

Library of Congress Cataloging-in-Publication Data
Hutton, Shirley.
   Pay yourself what you're worth.

   I. Direct selling.   I. deSwaan, Constance.
   II. Title.
   HF5438.25.H87   1988   658.8'4   87-19593
   ISBN 0-553-05249-7

Published simultaneously in the United States and Canada

Bantam Books are published by Bantam Books, a division of Bantam
Doubleday Dell Publishing Group, Inc. Its trademark, consisting of the
words "Bantam Books" and the portrayal of a rooster, is Registered in
U.S. Patent and Trademark Office and in other countries. Marca Regis-
trada. Bantam Books, 666 Fifth Avenue, New York, New York 10103.

PRINTED   IN   THE   UNITED   STATES   OF   AMERICA

DH   0 9 8 7 6 5 4 3

To my mother, Frances Nelson, and my late father William Nelson, whose love and discipline enabled me early on to understand that "if it is to be, it is up to me." Their spiritual strength—which they lived, spoke and "walked their words"—ultimately gave me strength, courage and direction.

To my children, Elizabeth, Chip, Bob, and Leslye, who, hopefully, realize now, or will one day see even more clearly, that I worked my many jobs to provide a better way of life for them while I struggled to find my own identity and meaning to life. I have discovered that parents are only children attempting to live an adult life, that they are people who are different from their children only because they've had a few more experiences.

To my ex-husband Joey, who in his own way, lovingly supported me. When I doubted myself, he always pointed to my triumphs and said, "You must be doing something right!"

Acknowledgments

To Mary Kay Ash, who created an opportunity for me and for all women in all walks of life and inspired us to find challenges and, ultimately, fulfillment. Her philosophy of life works in business as well as in our struggles to be loving wives and mothers. I believe, as she does, that women must keep their priorities in order, putting faith first, family second, and career third—and if any of these is out of order, nothing works.

To the Mary Kay Beauty Consultants from whom I still learn, the Sales Directors who willingly share ideas and give support, and to the other National Sales Directors who inspire me to achieve through their loving competition.

To my "offspring" Sales Directors, who took risks and followed me through this journey which has provided all of us with an extraordinary way of life.

To Connie deSwaan, who suggested I do this book and patiently collaborated with me on this venture, believing I could help others with what I knew about sales.

And to Linda Cunningham and Barbara Alpert, my editors, who made this book possible.

Table of Contents

Introduction

Years ago, a star football lineman was asked if he went through any ritual before going out on the field. He replied, "I don't like to jump from tall buildings before big games."

A friend recently told me this anecdote about John Campana, then playing for his college team. At first, Campana's clever put-down of superstitions made us laugh. Then it suddenly made me think. Here, a talented athlete had clearly *learned* the game, he'd *mastered* the rules, he understood *teamwork*, but he had something special, something that made him a star; he took *real* risks, real jumps into the fray. I'd be willing to bet he was a very *motivated* player—I can't imagine any champion reaching that height of success without some guiding inner force. He dared to go out there, to try what he knew to *reach a goal*, and, he was willing to take a few lumps to get there!

Campana's reply struck me at the moment. I'd just been talking about motivation and success with a few women on my "team" who were stalled at a crossroads selling with Mary Kay Cosmetics. I'd also met other women who were stuck for similar reasons—but they were hesitating about the career. These women *all* worried about succeeding, about failing, about taking risks, losing, losing *money*, making *enough* money, being rejected and getting spiritually "bruised," and about not making friends in the business. Those in the career already had learned the techniques of the selling game, but when they started to get somewhere, they froze—frightened to go on up another level, afraid that the price of success would be too much higher than the price of staying the same! They worried about getting every "move" right—every word of a sales presentation recited in the correct order and said in the most effective tone of voice. They were mentally leaping off tall buildings—and not landing on their feet—when I believed they should be imagining what it would be like to *live* at the top of one!

This book, then, is about landing on your feet—or *getting* on your feet—if you're just starting out in sales. It's a book about all of us: people who are remarkable because we have taken a chance on ourselves by using the opportunities available in direct sales. It's about all of you, too: people who are about to enter this exciting profession. This is a book filled with experiences that will show you, by example, what others in sales have learned—how they struggled, and how they triumphed. In my career, I've been given personal attention from friends I made in the company, direction from mentors like Mary Kay Ash, and good advice from success-oriented friends, all people with "something," and I want to pass their guidance along to you.

Mostly, this is a guidebook that can *teach* you to sell, show you how to approach people, tackle problems one at a time, explain why you must keep taking risks, why you must believe in yourself and develop the right attitude to keep going. In putting this book together, I've included a chapter on positive attitudes, getting motivated, and how to goal-set. Individual behavior is so complex that we may start out wanting success, but we trip ourselves up by worrying about everything but reaching that goal. We'll take a look at what some traps are, what needs to be done to eliminate them, and how to encourage winning strategies. These are the strategies that worked for me.

As you read through these pages, you'll see what it takes to be an *entrepreneur*—because once you sign up with a direct sales company, you're in your own business! The blessing of this industry is that you can set your own standards, determine how much money you want to make, and set your own hours. This book will help you learn, then, how to get sales to maintain and build your business. I've met people over the years who are content with earning "a little extra" and others who have always "thought big" from the second they joined a company. I am among the latter, if only because the opportunity was there and I could not imagine *not* taking it!

The direct selling business has been very good to me. My career, as with so many others in sales, does tell a "rags-to-riches" story, and it's one I want to share with you. I started out with Mary Kay Cosmetics. I'd had a wide variety of previous jobs. Each job provided me with some skill that I could later apply to winning in sales—whether it was attention to details, learning to deal with people, even getting over a fear of speaking to a large group. When I joined Mary Kay, I learned to sell products, but I also learned to sell myself and sell others on the career, too.

I've been in this business since 1973, not just selling beauty care, but helping people understand and learn the techniques of effective selling. I *believe sales ability can be learned.*

If you put your mind to it, you can sell anything—lipstick, vacuum cleaners, brass tacks, soft-soled shoes, or *crackers* to a thirsty man. The purpose of this book is to provide you with that kind of information, inspiration, and motivation. I want to capture your imagination by presenting the phenomenal possibilities and techniques to win in sales.

All you need to begin is a sense of excitement for the product and enough of a sense of adventure to allow you to take a few extra chances. I know you have it in you. Just think the best *of* yourself, and *for* yourself, then sell yourself on one of the greatest careers of the decade.

Let me first introduce myself, then introduce you to the industry. . . .

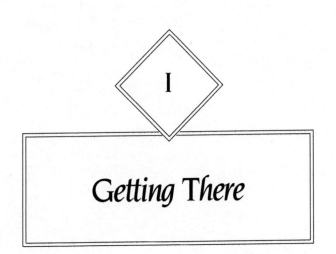

Getting There

Getting There

Getting There—
My Story

When you're successful, peo-
ple ask you questions about success: *How* did you do it? *Why*
did you do it? Do you really earn *all* that money yourself? How
do you keep the friends you made in your "poor" days? Do
you know a formula for success that could mean something to
me? What special "something" do you have—and how do I
get it, too?

I have always considered myself an ordinary woman who
has done extraordinary things. That's *my* something. I have
curiosity. Energy. I'm a risk taker. I have always believed that if
I wanted more out of life, it would be up to me to get it—and
that was okay. My family comes first, but I will make the time
for a career. I persist when I need to. I'll go the extra mile.

What makes me different is, perhaps, how I put together
all these qualities and apply them. Here's what I mean.

Years ago, I got a call from a recruit who implored me to
come down and speak at a Mary Kay meeting she was holding
in a few days. I was happy to help build her business in any

way I could, but she had called me at a rough time. I'd been working very hard, I was busy with some projects with my children, and I felt rushed. The meeting would be held in Rockford, Illinois, where my recruit lived, and I was still based in Minneapolis—which at the moment of her call was being blanketed by a classic midwestern snowstorm. I thought no but said yes, I'd be there.

A bumpy plane flight left me in Chicago, where I found my way to a railway station and bought my ticket to Shaumburg, Illinois, an hour away. There I was greeted by another consultant who had kindly volunteered to drive me an hour and a half further on to Rockford—this time, not through snow, but ice. I'd hit a second storm.

Miraculously, we arrived, chilled but safe, at the Ramada Inn where the meeting had been scheduled. I inquired at the desk for the Mary Kay meeting, but was told that it had been canceled. "No one could make it through the storm," the desk manager said. "We made it!" I replied.

Here's the rub: The recruit who had implored me to come to Illinois in the first place lived *two blocks* from the Inn!

This incident might have been good cause to get stomping mad and retrace my journey back without a second thought. But I took it with an almost fatalistic calm. It would have been easy to view this trip as a sad waste of time, effort, and money. "It's an impossible situation, but it has possibilities," a movie mogul once stated paradoxically about a film beset by problems. I took his wisdom to heart and faced *my* possibility—Carolyn, the consultant who'd braved the night with me.

As it turned out, the evening was productive. Over dinner I talked with her in depth about direct selling, we examined some difficulties she'd been facing, and, as a bonus, I got to make a valuable friend and ally.

Now, if we did an update on the women involved in this

fateful evening, I think you'd get a yet sharper picture of why some people with "something" succeed and others don't. The recruit who planned the meeting, along with the four women she invited, did not get much past their front doors in terms of career advancement. The consultant who braved the weather with me is still an active consultant with Mary Kay.

This is only one example of many similar situations I've faced on my way up. I've flown all over the country, meeting with success, but also with unexpected disasters! This particular incident really wasn't unusual for me and it certainly isn't unusual for those of us in direct sales. This "lost cause" can occur in some form in every salesperson's career—in as atmospherically dramatic conditions or under clearer skies. You'll confront a selling situation with all the "wrong" components—you're tired, you're rushed for time, the location is inconvenient, you don't know how reliable the others are—*but you show up because this is your career*. If you don't take it seriously, no one else will be accountable but you.

I loved this career from the beginning, and I showed up! As a result, it brought me great rewards, among them, self-confidence, a huge network of friends and associates who help and motivate me and each other, and a terrific income. Which leads me to the second category of questions people ask about my business: How can you sell lipstick? Do you really *like* the products? How can you get excited about makeup day in and day out? Can you really make a significant income? Doesn't a career in sales *embarrass* you?

My answers are simple:

I love what I sell.

I believe in the products.

I will always sell them with persistence, faith, and unflagging energy!

I'm unashamedly enthusiastic about what I do and it's

placed me number one in sales for three years in a row with Mary Kay. I sell lipstick, blusher, and facial masks, but, in truth, that's not the only exchange taking place. I also offer others the opportunity for the same kind of personal growth and recognition I've achieved when they choose to sell what I do. I could never have committed to sales so thoroughly had I not believed in the products and the high standards that are at the heart of the company. So, I'm not just selling a skin care line, but a career and a company philosophy.

This career has been one of the most gratifying experiences of my life. Right from the start I approached it wholeheartedly. I had to believe in myself and have an ongoing willingness to learn something new about selling and dealing with people every single day. I suffered setbacks, moments of grave doubt, awful frustration from rejection, but I stayed with it. My commitment to this career has yielded financial independence and the kind of self-esteem that comes from building a business at my own pace. It's given me personal enrichment from knowing I've succeeded at something I toiled hard for, planned with care, and carried out to the best of my abilities . . . as well as the joy, the highs, and the recognition and rewards from the company.

So, how *did* I do it? My objective was success from the day I put pen to paper and agreed to join Mary Kay. When I started out, I honestly didn't know what I was doing some of the time, improvising my way in and out of situations. Then, I had to overcome the poor image of "salesperson," a stereotype of either the pushy, foot-in-the-door type or the tired loser with an ashen complexion. I heard phones slamming down more often than not. Rejection is a big part of this business. I could have easily surrendered my career as the sun went down on another day of ten *no*'s and one *yes*, but I didn't. On my long trek upward, there were times when I'd rather have done anything than make another call or book another appointment to demonstrate products, but I kept moving! Every *yes* counted. They added up meteorically and made me a record holder with Mary Kay Cosmetics:

- ◆ I'm still the first and only Sales Director with an unmatched sales record of $1,300,000 in one year.

- ◆ I've won eight mink coats, the same number of pink Cadillacs, twelve diamond bumble bee pins (a symbol of the company), and a specially arranged $5,000 shopping spree at Neiman-Marcus in Dallas.

- ◆ In my very best *month*, I received the highest commission check the company *ever* paid anyone—$50,000—and it's still an unbeaten record!

- ◆ I've recruited (or recruited the recruits who recruited) about fifty thousand women, with about ten thousand remaining who are active.

- ◆ I've been first in sales three years in a row and have been frequently honored at ''seminar,'' a combination Oscar-type-awards ceremony and company celebration given by Mary Kay.

For someone who struggled by on not enough money most of her life, earning these sums and receiving honors were a triumph of tenacity and long hours paying off.

I grew up in a rented apartment over a movie theater in Willmar, Minnesota; my father worked for the railroad and my mother managed a dress shop. We were a family long on tradition, discipline, and love, but short on material privileges—no car, no backyard, very, very few extras. I married Joe Hutton when I was twenty years old and still in college. Joe began his career as a basketball player who early on opted to teach rather than continue with the Minneapolis Lakers. Ultimately, we had four children—two boys and two girls.

My work history is not quite as traditional. I've had tiresome jobs and glamorous jobs—and I've been working since the age of eleven, baby-sitting at a dime an hour, then employed as a maid for fifty cents an hour when I was a teenager, and teaching swimming for the Red Cross. An arms factory hired me after college, and I spent eight hours a day behind a desk as a clerk-typist. I've taught high school as a substitute teacher, been a fashion model (showroom and commercial photography) and eventually began doing TV commercials. I took buses to work, saving money by doing my own hair and makeup so I could treat myself to a secondhand car.

Exposure from those commercials was my first real break. Someone saw me and called to ask if I'd care to audition as cohost for Midday, a half-hour TV talk show based in Minneapolis. It took six callbacks with me doing six different interviews before I heard the good news that I'd be joining the team.

I was earning $11,000 a year at Midday (after four-and-a-half years there!) when a Mary Kay Beauty Consultant offered to give me a complimentary facial. My interest was minimal and, partially to put her off, I told Marilyn to be at my house at eight the next morning—the only time I had available all week. My saying yes was fateful! I liked the facial and began using the Mary Kay skin care line. For about eight months, I found myself recommending Mary Kay products to people, though I never considered selling it myself. But Marilyn had been taught at a training seminar to recruit her best customer. She did, and that was me!

I didn't think of myself as a likely candidate for direct sales but I knew the moment Marilyn opened the recruiting note-

book that the company appealed to me: there were no assigned territories, there were excellent tax benefits from
running a business from home, and I could set my own earning levels. I was attracted by the genuine support that came
from the sales directors and Mary Kay's own understanding of
women—that we need recognition for work well done and just
payment for the work we do well.

Some people look at the Mary Kay pink showcase of
products and see money, diamonds, travel, and achievement.
Others gaze woefully at the jars of makeup and see themselves fearful and unable to sell a thing—failing before they
even begin. I saw the magic and signed on.

Marilyn was good at what she did, letting me know she
thought I could fashion a sensational career in this business.
She saw my future and helped convince me that I'd succeed. I
believed her, and I believed in myself. I had nothing to lose. I
worked hard, and persisted. The first year, I earned about
$1,000 a month in sales *plus* I won two fur coats, my first bum-
ble bee pin, and numerous other prizes. My second year was
an improvement on these figures, but my third year looked
especially good—$60,000! From there, income increases
were less dramatic in span, but life-changing and ego-
enhancing. I remember hitting $100,000, then $125,000, then
eventually $200,000, $250,000 to $300,000, and one year, it
topped $400,000. This money was earned in *commissions* on
sales in my unit.

I reached these financial plateaus by taking one small step
at a time. Each time, my feet were firmly planted on the
ground, though others thought I was walking on eggs by going into a sales career. When I first signed up with Mary Kay,
reactions ranged from doubtful to very, very doubtful. My
husband thought I'd lost my mind, my daughter Elizabeth
was shocked, and the other three children more or less snick-

ered. Within the first few months of selling, I saw more gaping jaws than any dentist. Shirley Hutton was selling blushers—and loving it!

My first sales, ironically enough, were to my daughter Elizabeth and seven of her chums at college. (Elizabeth soon changed her opinion of the business and is now a high achiever with Mary Kay, too.) Since those initial sales in a Minnesota college dormitory, I've had skin care classes—our term for demonstration parties—at trailer courts, country cabins, singles' apartment complexes, and blueblood estates throughout the United States and Canada. I wanted to be *number one* and I followed every lead, no matter where. After two-and-a-half years of overlapping both careers, I left television to try for my goal. My fifth, sixth, and seventh year, I made it—I was in the top spot three times in a row!

I've been down and I've been up, and as the saying goes, up is better. The view from the top is vast, clear most of the time, and worth the climb because you did it yourself! To get there, you don't have to "pay the price," either. Instead, you change your priorities around and restructure your time to carry out your goal. And when you reach that goal, your self-esteem is high—high in the way it can only be from doing it yourself. No one can give you self-esteem. It comes from within, from accomplishment, from belief in an idea, and just enough grit to keep going during hard times.

Direct sales has been good to me. I saw what I needed to do to succeed and planned it step by step. It broke down this way:

◆ Book demonstration "skin care classes"

◆ Recruit business partners and train them

- Keep sight of my goal at all times and understand that setbacks and rejection will be a part of it

- Remain conscientious and disciplined

- Be persistent and good-humored

- Give myself time to build a volume business

- Ask others for help and guidance

This book will take you through all these steps and show you what they mean. First, let me define direct sales for you.

Demystifying Direct Sales

Direct sales is simply a means of approaching customers either on a person-to-person basis or through prearranged groups—alternately called "at-home party plans," "skin care classes," "demonstration parties"—or through personal appointments to sell products or to recruit others to sell. Direct sales offers convenience with an emphasis on personal service, and, of course, the choice to build a great career selling the very products you like using. Discovery Toys, Doncaster, Shaklee, Fuller Brush, and Mary Kay are just a few of the hundreds of direct sales companies where the salesperson goes "direct" to the client.

Direct sales as a career will offer you:

- an exceptional opportunity to build a career on your own terms.

♦ a way to increase monthly income while working the hours that most suit you.

♦ a deep sense of accomplishment and the joy of recognition for work well done. (Annual company "seminars" can be as inspiring as the Academy Awards or a beauty pageant.)

♦ a chance to set up your own business, with all the accompanying benefits—self-esteem, financial success, no bosses (but the one you face in the mirror on a daily basis) and tax breaks, too.

♦ a choice in the kind of product you'll be dealing with.

♦ a chance to take your business with you if you relocate—an option available from many direct sales companies.

♦ the ability to have a career and rear your children—direct sales lets you work from your own home at your own pace.

Most of all, direct sales is a profession for the future, available to anyone with an enterprising spirit. The potential is limitless! Determine how much you want to earn, lay out the plan, and go for it! That's exactly what I did. So, in fact, have the nearly six million others who've joined the growing number of direct sales companies, which will do about $8 billion in sales this year.

Not everyone in direct sales strives for six-figure incomes. Many people are content with a smaller but significant addition to the monthly income in a one- or two-salary family. Married, divorced, or single women often ease out of office jobs and into their own businesses—building businesses, in fact, in their spare time, as I did at first. Husbands, also, are inspired to join a direct sales company when their wives do well—an interesting phenomenon in direct sales. Though once almost exclusively a man's domain, direct sales now supports about two men to every eight women!

Are you eligible? Yes!

Direct sales companies don't discriminate. You can be a thirty-year-old mother of three with no work experience, a forty-year-old optician, a twenty-two-year-old teacher. You needn't worry about possessing a college degree or exceptional good looks. Talk-show hostesses (I was one in my prior career), performers, women returning to work after years at home, retirees searching for a new occupation that's not too physically demanding, executives who'd love to leave the grind of offices—they can all be found somewhere in direct sales companies, most of them devoting only a few hours a day to selling. In fact, the Direct Selling Association in Washington estimates that *most* salespersons are working part-time—about 88.1 percent of them, while only 11.9 percent consider direct sales a full-time job.

Then there's a more fascinating breakdown of who's in direct sales from Association statistics: They estimate that about 80 percent of the salesforce are women, 15 percent are minorities, 10 percent are disabled, and 5 percent are over sixty-five years old. The bare facts reveal that anyone can sell and that women, in particular, are choosing direct sales in ever-increasing numbers to supplement their incomes or are making a career of it.

The structure of direct sales is so unique that it can work for a part-timer who's satisfied with bringing in an extra $50 a week or the ambitious careerist who's determined to build an ongoing, growing five- and six-figure income. I've spoken to people who began with direct sales when the company they'd chosen had pretty much just "opened for business." These risk takers found incredible earning opportunities. Then again, there are people who have joined older, established companies and found happiness at a less dramatic earning level.

Direct sales is also an exciting way for women and men to enter the work force—and stay there on their own terms.

Anyone can learn the business. It will take faith in yourself, and a willingness to learn and teach others. It requires that you voluntarily establish or attend support groups where you can exchange ideas, get positive reinforcement, and develop personally. When you're the boss, you work alone. Meeting with others in the business keeps you in touch with new techniques to see and, most importantly, gets you *motivated*.

I anticipate your next question: How does direct sales actually work?

At its simplest level, direct sales eliminates the "middlemen" between the consumer and the manufacturer. Who are these middlemen? They are *costs*, or people incurring costs, such as overhead, advertising, shipping, wholesalers, packaging, and so on. Middlemen add to the cost of the product. Period. The main difference between direct sales and retail sales (a department store, for example) is the critical one: The *profit* in your business goes to you and the other salespeople who work for you, rather than into the bank accounts of all those intermediaries.

Here's an example: Mary Kay is one of the giants in direct sales, specializing in skin care products and cosmetics. You can't buy Mary Kay products at the supermarket, and you'll very seldom see the company's products advertised on television. So if you want a high-quality skin cleanser, you'd have to contact a Mary Kay beauty consultant to fill the order for you. If you want a bottle of shampoo that's advertised nationally, you'll find it in nearly every store that sells soap. You'll also find the price affected by the many stages this bottle of shampoo goes through to get to all those stores.

So, why buy Mary Kay skin cleanser or Discovery Toys or Shaklee vitamins, anyway? Products you purchase through these direct sales companies not only offer the convenience of home shopping, but they're often higher quality than advertised brands. In many cases, companies use a percentage of the profits for research to improve the product. And don't forget this: You're buying products at wholesale prices and selling them at retail.

I'll describe a few marketing plans for you in the upcoming chapter so you can see how commissions may be earned. Marketing plans for the company you choose will determine *how* you'll earn, and your own energy and enthusiasm will determine how *much*. In a number of these companies, you'll discover that how much will also depend on how *many* people you can recruit into your business. Why? By motivating and recruiting others to sell and start businesses, too, you'll earn a percentage on what they've sold.

To give you an idea of what this means in terms of numbers: I earn anywhere from 4 to 25 percent on all wholesale sales by the people I've recruited and the people *they've* recruited. (I'll tell you more about this process later on.) The total number of people who are somehow connected to me is about eleven thousand! That's people, again, not dollars—people whose output, commitment, and energy affects my income.

A Few Words on Selling

Those of us plying our trade in sales have a few poor examples to live down. The good news is that about 65 percent of all direct sales representatives generally work within their own communities and uphold their integrity with the people they sell to. We are your neighbors! Many sales representatives who aren't limited by assigned territories thrive on referrals from hometown friends and customers for *new* customers (and recruits) who live out of state or in another county. Therefore, those of us who've made direct sales our part-time or full-time career need those people to trust us—and they do.

Your "sales image" is up to you. When you become a salesperson, it's up to you to be gracious, honest, and dignified. You'll always fit in.

Fitting in brings up another question about the personal aspect of sales—the sense of oneself as a salesperson. Do you think you're right for sales? Do you think you're good in sales? Can you feel confident about actually saying, "I'm in sales"? When the beauty consultant who eventually recruited me asked if I wanted to join Mary Kay, I answered automatically, "Of course not!" I didn't see myself in that role. I had a view of sales (and salespeople) that focused on the buyer's end of the scale. I perceived sales as a transaction initiated by someone who either stood behind a shop counter or called and tried to sell you magazine subscriptions over the phone. This was sales and those were salespeople. It had nothing to do with me, really. But, believing in the Mary Kay company—after using the products for nearly a year—I signed up. It immediately changed my perception of sales, selling, and my place in the scheme of things. It's amazing what the emphasis in a simple point of view can do for your income and self-esteem. This is what I want to share with you in this book.

Everyone sells—and that starts with how you sell yourself. Few of us like to think we're packaged, tagged with a price, and marketed—and of course, we do not sell ourselves in quite this calculated a manner. But the truth is that we do sell our opinions to others in varying degrees of persuasiveness. We tout a restaurant, a movie, a product, a lifestyle, urging others to enjoy it as much as we do. More personally, we communicate to others who we are, what we care about, what we do and don't want in our lives.

That's sales, too.

So though not all selling is inspired by a profit motive, whether we like it or not, we're all salespeople. And the truth is that we can sell anything to anybody else when we've sold ourselves on it. "Anything" includes a product, a theory, or who we are. If we believe in it, we can sell it! The only "sales" experience you need to succeed in direct selling is an ability to talk to others, to talk enthusiastically about what you're doing to build your business, and to think positively about yourself. As you read this book, you'll discover how to strengthen the communication skills you already possess and learn new ones so you can feel good about what you're doing.

Personal gratification and financial rewards come from success in this business. Direct selling may alter your lifestyle as dramatically as it changed mine. Higher earnings through direct selling (even part-time, the way I started), bring relief from the stress of living within a tight or seriously limiting budget. Extra money brings *freedom.* You can afford to make choices formerly outside your income bracket. You'll be able to make spending decisions based on desire—the difference between vacationing in the Greek Islands or visiting relatives for an extended weekend.

If you are a woman married to a man who earns what you both consider a good income (or the reverse), direct selling not only adds to your income, but can lower your tax rates. (There's a chapter ahead on how this business benefits you through tax breaks.) If you're single, you can build a business on a full- or part-time basis while increasing your network of friends.

Direct selling gives you a chance to work on your own, at your own pace, at your own hours, at home or at others' homes, seeing people you want to see, and feeling a sense of accomplishment. You'll discover that while money-making might have brought you to the career, your gains will be greater with personal growth. You'll learn to handle rejection—to let go of those who say no—and move forward. A career in direct sales teaches you to plan a more productive life—you'll be setting and meeting goals and tasting success. But *you* need to take that step and discover the direct selling company that will suit you—the company that makes the product you believe in. Combine this with your ability to create a profession that's going to change your life, and you can only win. And you alone will determine how far to go and what you want. No one will lean on you to produce. You can go as far as your motivation takes you—and believe me, it's easily possible to become motivated.

Direct sales could be the new career with the kind of benefits you may be looking for. It means being your own boss, establishing a business where you need little experience and less capital to get started. It offers diverse product lines—cosmetics, clothing, decorative accessories, houseware specialties, home-security systems, vitamins, and crafts. It means forming support teams where you can meet challenges and goals, and start your way to higher income. Direct sales has it all—recognition for work well done, totally flexible hours, financial rewards, and most of all, the kind of personal growth that allows you to put the career together effectively.

To succeed in the business, you need to get an idea of the kinds of companies you'd be working with and how they market their products. So let's begin there. . . .

A Close-Up Look
at Direct Sales

Among the five million or so of us in direct sales, we've probably been in a few hundred million homes, toting sample kits or catalogs, earning a handsome portion of the total of eight billion dollars estimated in retail sales volume that direct sales companies tallied last year. We sell clothing and vacuum cleaners, nutritional supplements and cosmetics, jewelry, and educational materials. Most of us are happy for the extra cash, and some of us, fired by ambition with far-reaching goals, set long-range plans with a company.

It's not unusual for direct salespeople to stumble into the business on the way to another job. Few plan on an unsalaried sales career. But there's one thing about direct selling—almost everyone knows someone who's in the business. It's an occupation that's as familiar to us as any other we could mention, but it can seem inaccessible. Often, until people actually sign up to sell (and recruit others), they don't understand how eligible they are or how much fun sales can be.

Sales is the career of the 1980s and, as economic futurists see it, about seven out of ten people may be in their own business by the late 1990s. The entrepreneurial spirit is more fervent than ever. Because hours and work schedules are so flexible, more women than ever are joining salesforces to *supplement* incomes while they raise families. They often discover they possess a talent to sell and sell with brilliance. There are few businesses that can promise anyone—man or woman— with no special education and training that with persistence, energy, and application of goal-setting, he or she can earn over $100,000 a year. And, because of the many earning possibilities through various systems including *reputable* "multi-level" payment plans, income can be even greater over the years. Imagine earning a percentage on sales made by those people you recruit, and the people they recruit, and so on. It's a remarkable opportunity.

Most people already have brushed shoulders with someone in direct sales—perhaps even attended a meeting, or invited a salesperson into their homes, or participated in home demonstration parties. Direct sales companies shouldn't be strangers to us at all. Stanhome and Tupperware made the home party famous, while the names Avon and Fuller Brush may forever prompt us to hear the sound of a doorbell ringing. May Kay's achievers announce their presence in a fleet of pink cars, while *Encyclopaedia Britannica* is synonymous with scholarly authority.

Choosing a direct sales company to work for can be problematic, especially for someone who's never sold before. Most people select a company because they like using the products they buy from "distributors" (each company prefers its own term for salesperson) and they agree to be recruited. Others of us may know of a company by reputation, and after investigating them further, discover that the opportunities are compatible with our needs.

The Direct Selling Association, a Washington, D.C.-based association that sets operating and ethical standards for member companies, reported what categories of products were the most popular in terms of the number of sales. The summary for 1984 looked like this:

Products Sold—Domestic	Percent of Sales
Cosmetics/Fragrances/Skin care	35.44%
Decorative accessories	18.42
Nutritional products/Beverages/Food	12.82
Home appliances	9.29
Other	1.03
House/Kitchenware	.69
Household/Auto care products	7.31
Jewelry	5.19
Educational publications	4.76
Crafts/Hobbies/Toys	2.47
Home enhancement	.00
Clothing	.91
Cookware/Tableware	.54
Animal care products and foods	.26
Home technology	.15
Photo album plans	.32
Shoes	.10
Buying club/Service	.27
Self-Improvement/vocational training programs	.03

Method of Selling	Percent of Sales
Individual one-to-one contact	78.90%
Party plan	21.10

("Party plans" involve a sales presentation given by a salesperson to a group of guests who will hopefully buy the product. The party is most typically given by someone asked to "host" it by the salesperson. I'll talk more on party plans later on.)

If we add this all up in product categories, we'd see a trend toward an increase in sales of home and family care products with personal care products second on the list. For 1984 the percentages broke down like this:

Product Categories	Percent of Sales
Personal care	33.52%
Home and family care products and services (such as vacuum cleaners, detergents, etc.)	48.55
Leisure and educational products	8.25
Home enhancement (such as novelty items, like wall plaques, picture frames, etc.)	2.25
Miscellaneous (includes insurance and buying clubs)	7.43

There are over one hundred companies in the Direct Selling Association—companies who've met certain standards of integrity in marketing, production, and sales plans. In addition, there are hundreds of others around who aren't affiliated with the Association, but who may be legitimate. Perhaps they are too new or it's their personal preference not to join. My belief is that you'll be safer with an affiliated company— you're sure of its being reputable.

How do we choose which company to join? Following is a sampling of what eight companies—selling a diversity of products—have to offer the new recruit. A number of companies feel that they cannot offer information about what the "average earnings" are for their salespeople, for example, believing the figures may be misconstrued as a company *promise* of income. And, with the different income goals and time devoted by salespersons, "averages" can sometimes be quite misleading. Otherwise, we've tried to be as comprehensive as possible. When information is missing, therefore, it should be taken to mean that the company declined to answer with an exact figure.

Amway

It's one of the world's largest personal selling companies operating in America and about forty other countries. Co-founded in 1959 by Richard DeVos and Jay Van Andel (in the basements of both men's homes), the company has now grown so huge that it supports about seven thousand employees and nearly one million distributorships! Amway researches and manufactures nearly all its own hundreds of products, including the original Liquid Organic Cleaner Concentrate, which launched them. The Amway name is in home care, housewares, nutrition and diet, personal care, and commercial life. They've also got a special shopping catalog that offers over four thousand brand name goods, also sold through distributors.

General guidelines:
Initial fee: Sales and product kit, $82; distributorship renewal fee, $15 annually
Average earnings: Not available
Price range for merchandise: Thousands of items range from $3.00 up to $4,000 (for a solar disc)
Assigned territories: None
Type of plan: One-on-one or small groups
Training program: Yes; there's also additional training for a fee of $25 for eight hours of instruction

Sales meetings: Depends on sponsor, but recommended on a weekly basis
Payment format: Commissions
Bonuses or incentives: Yes

Discovery Toys

Nine years ago, Lane Nemeth, a thirty-year-old mother of a baby girl and director of a California day-care center, borrowed $50,000 and began a toy business in her garage that mushroomed into a $40-million success story! Every Discovery Toy is designed to develop a child's physical or intellectual ability—"Child's play is really child's work, and it's up to the parent to provide the right tools." This guiding philosophy has motivated 12,000 consultants to work with this innovative company—and they're projecting a need for about 100,000 more consultants to join them. The product line changes about twice a year and consultants are briefed on new products through training sessions.

General guidelines:
Initial fee: Kit: two models available with continuing and new products at either $115 or $190
Average earnings: Not available
Price range for merchandise: 75 percent of toys are under $10; highest price, $29.98
Assigned territories: None
Type of plan: Party plan with at-home demonstrations
Training: Encouraged to be trained by manager
Sales meetings: Yes
Quotas: To remain active, there's a minimum sales requirement of about $20 per month

Payment format: Multilevel marketing
Bonuses or incentives: Cars, trips, cash awards

Doncaster

This North Carolina-based company was founded fifty-two years ago by the Tanner family with the idea of marketing designer clothes for women "who never have to enter an apparel store to dress well." Customers view each Doncaster collection and select styles, then order them custom-cut in colors and fabric of their choice; Doncaster hand-finishes details. Their lines are meant to carry over year to year—"investment dressing" to the trade—and sell for considerably less than or at prices comparable to well-known designers. The "fashion consultant" (their term for salesperson) is an independent contractor who can purchase Doncaster wardrobes at substantial savings besides earning on a commission basis.

General guidelines:
Initial fee: None. Doncaster gives a consultant six months to "get on her feet," offering a sample book that's available for one week. Since they show a "fall/winter" line and a "spring/summer" line, the second season the salesperson is with the company, there's a minimum charge of $22.
Average earnings: Not available
Price range for merchandise: Depends on style and fabric. $50–$100 is average for pants; wool suits (semi-custom made), $500; $250 for a skirt, $125 for blouses; $175 for a "Traditions" line dress.
Assigned territories: Yes
Type of plan: Recommended private appointments for not more than two people
Training: Yes, by manager

Payment format: Basic commissions, then greater bonus payments over a certain level of sales
Bonuses or incentives: Yes

Encyclopaedia Britannica

The first three-volume set was published in 1768 and from this simple beginning, Britannica reigns as the oldest continuously published reference work in the English language. Dedicated to the premise that education and knowledge are fundamental to improving the condition of mankind, the company has hired scholars and authorities over the centuries to contribute to its pages, including Albert Einstein, George Bernard Shaw, and Lyndon Johnson. The 30-volume set, probably in every American library and in millions of homes, has its own folklore—George Washington paid $6 for a pirated version after failing in an attempt to win a set in a lottery; and Prince Aly Khan bought a set in the most expensive binding. International editions include a 28-volume edition in Japanese and a 22-volume edition in Italian; there's also a 12-volume children's Britannica and many other foreign language versions. The books are sold by representatives, but the company has increased its exposure by selling in large shopping malls and theme parks.

General guidelines:
Initial fee: None. There's a condensed one-volume sample version at no cost.
Average earnings: "Fluctuates"
Price range for merchandise: Initial set is approximately $1,249, the Heirloom set, $1,499. Fancy bindings and limited editions priced higher.
Assigned territories: Yes. Salesforce works within assigned districts.

Type of plan: Person-to-person in home and retail outlets
Training: Trained by people at the district level
Sales meetings: Yes.
Payment format: Commission
Bonuses or incentives: Yes

The Fuller Brush Company

The only direct sales company that can boast two feature films with its name in the title (*The Fuller Brush Man* with Red Skelton and *The Fuller Brush Woman* with Lucille Ball), this eighty-year-old company is one of the first to come to mind when thinking door-to-door sales. At one time, Fuller Brush hired men only, but now about 80 percent of the salesforce is women. And though door-to-door is still a popular method of sales, many salespeople organize home shows instead. The original line of twelve household brushes, designed and made by Alfred C. Fuller, founder of the company, has grown to include homecare products, industrial chemical cleaners, brushes, and soaps. About sixty or so products are added each year with quarterly catalogs covering the range of wares.

General guidelines:
Initial fee: It will cost either $29 or $45 for one sample kit including a catalog and brochure and merchandise; the $45 kit has the "first line of merchandise."
Average earnings: The company estimates $8 an hour on the average, $12–$15 for someone more motivated. Bonus rewards from referrals can also be earned.
Price range for merchandise: $2–$35, with the average $6–$10
Assigned territories: Yes
Type of plan: Door-to-door with optional home shows

Training: The company recommends training, done by the field manager who recruited the salesperson
Sales meetings: Once every four weeks
Quotas: None
Payment format: Commissions; salary and bonuses for managers who work at company offices
Bonuses or incentives: Gifts, bonds, cash, trips, depending on level of achievement

Jafra Cosmetics, Inc.

Janice Eldredge Day and her husband Frank Day combined their names and talents a bit over thirty years ago to found one of the more successful, personally run direct sales companies in America. The Gillette Company is now its "parent," but Jafra continues to maintain the unique and separate identity that is its trademark. From Jafra's modest beginnings in Malibu, California, the Days built an organization that now offers its special entrepreneurial opportunity to women in eighteen countries. The Days' original premise for Jafra was to provide high-quality products and low-key sales programs that emphasize company supportiveness. Over the years, the Jafra philosophy has changed the lives of thousands of women who discovered a career through "party plan" sales. Jafra's original line of skin care products and fragrances have expanded to include nail care.

General guidelines:
Initial fee: For $95, consultants purchase a demonstration case which includes essential products and sales aids for initial classes.
Average earnings: Depends on the consultant's sales
Price range for merchandise: $4.50 to $35

Assigned territories: No

Type of plan: In-home skin care and nail care classes

Training: The company provides training aids and encourages training through managers and class observation. In 1987, Jafra launched the Jafra Training Institute, an on-going personal program to develop leadership and management skills.

Sales meetings: Weekly, whenever possible.

Quotas: To maintain wholesale privileges, consultants must place an order every sixty days.

Payment format: Consultant and managers are independent contractors who order directly from the company. Managers are also paid on commissions.

Bonuses or incentives: Gifts, cash, trips, cars—depending on the level of achievement.

Mary Kay Cosmetics, Inc.

The first products were packaged in blue, but no one remembers—pink symbolizes the Mary Kay company and all its spectacular opportunities for women and men. Mary Kay Ash founded her company in 1963 after a long career in sales. She wanted to create an organization that allowed women achievement and generously rewarded them for work well done, a company run on her moral beliefs in God, family, and the golden rule. The first storefront in a Dallas office building sold wigs and her special skin care line. It was begun with her son, Richard Rogers, a marketing genius and now chairman of the company. Mary Kay Cosmetics has grown rapidly from its original $5,000 investment and about 10 consultants to about 150,000 consultants and directors in 1987. The Mary Kay items of skin care and "glamour" (cosmetics) number about forty, allowing each consultant to easily stock the entire line.

Mary Kay has added a "Color Awareness" program, which helps customers coordinate makeup with wardrobe as well as a nail-care line.

General guidelines:

Initial Fee: $85 demonstration case

Average earnings: $10–$50 an hour. (Top level national sales directors can earn from $50,000–$400,000 a year.)

Price range for merchandise: $5–$25 per item, around $20 for fragrances

Assigned territories: None

Type of plan: "Party," with recommendation of no more than six women per "skin care class" (Mary Kay's term for party), or by private appointment

Training program: Free weekly training for beginners, ongoing local and national seminars

Sales meetings: Suggested for every Monday

Quotas: Must order $180 wholesale every five months to remain "active"

Payment format: Resale profits up to 50% (the difference between wholesale and retail); override commissions on salesperson's "active" recruits sales of 4–12%; additional commissions as salesperson progresses upward.

Bonuses or incentives: Cash, jewelry, cars, trips, furs, depending on achievement

The Shaklee Corporation

Dr. Forrest C. Shaklee and his sons, Forrest Jr. and Raleigh, built their company with a commitment to the golden rule and excellence in the field of nutritional products. Shaklee is now one of the new direct sales companies who have gone public and is listed on the New York Stock Exchange. Shaklee products—manufactured with the motto "products in harmony with nature and good health"—include a skin care and cosmetics line, multivitamins, a "slim line" nutritional supplement, and many personal care and household items—including shampoo, cleaners, toothpaste, and hand creams. The company has incentive plans for winning cars, trips, and extra earnings. Shaklee (along with Mary Kay, Amway, and others) has gone international, with distributors in Japan, Germany, the United Kingdom, and Australia.

General guidelines:

Initial fee: $15 for a distributor kit which includes a business sales manual and product information.

Average earnings: The company estimates that by putting in 10–15 hours a week, a distributor can earn a bonus of $460 a month.

Price range for merchandise: $1.95–$20.00 (Some products can be purchased in bulk sizes for more than $20.)

Assigned territories: None.

Type of plan: Most sell person to person, but the company doesn't object to distributors hosting small meetings at their option.

Training: Training encouraged for programs in business management, nutrition, diet management, color evaluation (for cosmetics), and skin care. Programs vary and can be conducted by professional makeup artists, by home office personnel, or field people trained by the company using corporate materials.

Sales meetings: Encouraged but not mandatory.

Quotas: To remain active, distributors are asked to buy $50 worth of products in one of every three months.

Payment format: Multilevel marketing.

Bonuses or incentives: Luxury international trips, cars, and other prizes for achievement.

Three of the categories we need to examine with a bit of scrutiny are **average earnings, assigned territories**, and **payment format**. Average earnings will probably fluctuate, because it is the scope of your sales territory, if any; the marketing plan of the company and the time and effort devoted that truly determine what you can earn.

A policy of assigning territories where you can or cannot sell, will, I think, eventually restrict your earning power. When the market you can tap, is, literally, worldwide, as with companies offering *un*assigned territories, it's a good idea to go with them and connect with as many people as you can. I've traveled this country and Canada to recruit people, and I know my business would not have been as strong if I'd been limited to, say, one corner of Minnesota.

There are a few other advantages to *un*assigned territories that experienced direct salespeople learn to appreciate. If a salesperson (or his/her spouse) must relocate for a job, the move does not have to affect the salesperson's income. He (or she) can still sell to the same retail customers, still recruit people out of the old location, and they can now pick up more income by selling and recruiting from a new home base. You can see how assigned territories might limit salespeople. If you move *out* of the territory, you may sacrifice your business. Once in a new area, you'd have to start all over!

Many direct selling companies with unassigned territories now have "adoption" systems. The newly relocated salesperson is "adopted" right into a new fold—she can attend a local sales director's meetings and be introduced to the area and get some valuable information and orientation to start her off again. Fuller Brush, Doncaster, and *Encyclopaedia Britannica* pay a commission on sales, and reward salespeople for referrals, but you do *not* earn any additional or ongoing percentages for sales made by anyone you've recruited. Discovery Toys, Amway, Shaklee, and Mary Kay do reward salespeople for sales made by others recruited into the business, and each has a different payment scale. The scale varies in percentages of commissions from company to company, but is based on essentially the same theory.

Because marketing plans, including "multilevel" marketing for a number of well-known companies, are complex and need a few diagrams to be explained clearly, I've gone into a longer discussion of it later in this chapter. Basically, though, this marketing structure involves a unique payment system that's based on one or more levels of salespeople. The amount of money someone can earn is determined this way: The salesperson makes profits from her own retail sales business, and to it she adds commission dollars on sales made by the people she sponsors into the company (recruits) and, depending on the company, her recruits' recruits. In most, those commissions depend on the recruited person's becoming an active seller of the company's products. There is no payment for the act of recruiting itself, to discourage "headhunting."

There is actually no absolute across-the-board definition of multilevel marketing that every company using this payment system abides by. However, it is of utmost importance that you understand the distinguishing points from company to company when you sign with one. In the Mary Kay company, for example, *every* beauty consultant, when recruited, pays *wholesale* prices to the company *only,* for products she sells at *retail* cost. So while Mary Kay has *no* levels of wholesalers, where recruits buy products from the person who sponsored them, rather than directly from the company, such others as Amway and Shaklee *do.*

Numerous companies sell their products through "party" plans, though they may have originally established their products by selling them on a one-to-one basis. Party plans are a popular pastime in some communities, especially where there are many young mothers, retirees, women wanting to get back into the business world, literally a few hours at a time. Party plans work like this: A salesperson contacts a friend or a friend of a friend and asks her to host a party. The hostess is given a list of basic rules: Parties must start on time, the room should be neat and well-lighted, and any limitations such as the number of guests so each woman can get the personal service and attention of the salesperson. Finally, the hostess is told how long the party will last, and asked to set things up so no children, dogs, or spouses wander in.

The sociability of the party plans adds to the pleasure of buying and selling, plus the hostess of a party may get a small percentage of the evening's sales. Usually, the hostess doesn't have to join the company to get that percentage, although a good salesperson might try to recruit her! Of course, there's a bit of work to planning a party, and it's the salesperson's responsibility to coach the hostess to get the most out of an evening.

Other companies who favor the tradition of home parties are Sarah Coventry (jewelry), Natural Impressions (a new company specializing in electroplated jewelry made with real leaves, shells, and twigs), Home Interiors and Gifts (a Dallas-based company specializing in home accessories), and Princess House (another company specializing in decorative home accessories and crystal.

Before you join a company, however, you should be aware of a few other important points:

What to Avoid When Choosing a Company

The first thing many people think or say when direct sales is mentioned, is "pyramids." While pyramid schemes are ille-

gal in most states, many marketing plans are legitimate enterprising systems of earning money—and are *not* pyramids.
Because the description of how various marketing plans work
sounds like the physical structure of a pyramid, people tend to
confuse the good with the bad.

Let me explain.

Pyramids rely on the dreamers of this world, for pyramid
schemes are designed to get investors to put in a chunk of
money, say $500 or more, for *nothing* in return. That is, no
product. If you're new in the game, you enter at one of the
bottom slots of the pyramid. To make a profit, you must sponsor others into the pyramid and they must pay you to get in.
In other words, you're just paying for the right to then turn
around and find recruits who'll pay *you* to get in. Eventually,
you hope to bring in enough people, up to the point where
you supposedly make your fortune.

This is called a "naked pyramid" scheme, and it's well
named—you can get stripped of your money. It's one of two
garden variety pyramids, this being the no-product type. It's a
cash-only pyramid, the likes of which swept California and
New York in flash floods about five years ago. It was estimated that about $100 million changed hands on the West
Coast and the fervent pyramid players in New York were coming up fast and furious when the pyramid toppled. Entering
into a no-product pyramid makes you poorer while the early
promoters of the scheme get richer.

The second species of pyramid actually offers a product,
but the point is not only to make a profit by selling directly to
a consumer. Instead, one salesperson sells to another level of
salesperson for a profit, who then in turn sells to another level
for his or her profit . . . until the bottom salesperson must
finally sell to a consumer to make the final profit. When dealing with this kind of profit structure, it's important to under-

stand what you have to do to move up to higher profit levels.

The Direct Selling Association Report on multilevel marketing listed some "red flags" of pyramiding.

You should look out for:

♦ Exaggerated or unsupported earnings claims used in recruiting. (One such claim will say, for example, that you can earn $200,000 a year selling their product. They may neglect to mention that it may take *ten years* to build up your business to make this amount. Then again, they might be promoting inflated numbers to lure you in. You can ask them for proof of income earnings—if they're a legitimate company they'll usually have a company magazine, newspaper, or monthly circular featuring high earners.)

♦ "Large" start-up fees or costs.

♦ Recruiting based on sponsoring others without emphasizing product sales.

♦ Loading new recruits with big inventories.

♦ Inadequate inventory "buy-back" policy.

You should know the company's buy-back policy before you sign up—in case circumstances force you to change occupations. You may want to return your inventory rather than sell it off to make your money back. Each company should let you know, in writing, what its particular buy-back policy is. Some companies give you only two weeks to return your inventory while others give you up to a year to get a refund on the merchandise you bought from them at wholesale prices. The Direct Selling Association suggsts that "inadequate" buy-back policies allow returns for a very short time after purchase, or only refund less than 90 percent of the cost of the merchandise to the salesperson.

In trying to decide which direct marketing company to join, you should do a thorough investigation.

You'll know some companies by reputation since they seem to be so much a part of mainstream American economy. You might have heard the names of others, but don't really know much about how they operate. Where do you go for answers?

Companies that have been around at least for a few years will be easier to investigate. They'll have offices, distributors, and retail customers. Write to these companies for information, annual reports, and a description of their full line of products. To check on a company's legitimacy, honesty, and track record, write to The Direct Selling Association in Washington (address in the back of the book) and ask what they know of a company. If they haven't heard of it, they may be able to refer you to a state business bureau which may be able to supply you with some information.

By doing your own investigative work you will save time and money in the end. Some companies may look great in the beginning, appearing to have the perfect product, great packaging, and high commission promises. But with careful examination, they may not look so good after all. Years ago, a diet product had a meteoric rise, but before long fizzed out in its own stratospheric hype. Marketing a get-thin-fast diet powder that sold on a get-rich-quick commission plan sounded great to both its planners and the salespeople who signed up to share in this marketing scheme. When the diet was publicly shown to be nutritionally inadequate, the company went bankrupt leaving many commission obligations unpaid.

This cautionary tale isn't in any way meant to turn you

away from joining a fledgling direct selling company. Rather, I urge you to be alert to company strategies that may sound very tantalizing but will not satisfy you in the end.

Direct Marketing Simplified

Direct marketing enables you to earn money in three distinct ways.

Step 1: You can retail the product only—that is, buy it at wholesale cost and sell it at retail price. As a consultant (or distributor or whatever your entry level title is), you order products either through the person who sponsored you into the company or directly from the company itself. You can use the products yourself and/or sell them to friends, relatives, whomever. You'll make a profit on these products, but the amount you earn won't be as great as if you go on to the next level.

Step 2: You decide to move up a slot to "management"—or whatever title your particular company designates for this second level. When you're in "management," you can sell your products (just as you did in step one) and also recruit others into the company to sell. Your income will be higher because you'll be earning commissions on what they sell. At this point, you're profiting from your own retail trade and the wholesale sales of your recruits. The next step up can be the most exciting.

Step 3: You can "duplicate" your business. Here's where you can take the opportunity and make a *lot* of money—and it's also where the "pyramid" confusion comes in. Duplicating—alternately called "spinning off" or having "offspring"—makes direct marketing very unique. Basically, it's getting someone whom you've recruited into your organization to achieve as you have and move up into "management." Then she, too, becomes an "offspring" and develops someone in her own organization to move up into management, and so on, down the line. You'll see how this works very shortly.

Starting Out: Why You Want to Recruit and Build a Business

Some direct selling companies operate on payment policies based on levels that go two, three, four, or sometimes five levels deep. There is not an infinite line downward for *you* to profit from directly. There is, however, an endless possibility of increasing your earnings *laterally*. This means you are not limited to the number of people you can personally recruit and add to your circle. The more people you recruit, the more people *they* can sponsor who can then sponsor others. This payment process will be further clarified for you in the upcoming discussion.

Each company operates with a "marketing plan" or "performance schedule" that will describe how you earn greater commissions and what your title will be as you move up— supervisor, director, coordinator, national sales director, key coordinator, diamond distributor, or whatever the company designates. How you earn and the title you win will be determined by either group (unit) sales volume and/or personal sales volume, the number of recruits you sponsor within a certain amount of time, and how long you maintain these numbers.

Your success depends upon the energy you put into selling and recruiting others into your organization. The greater the number of people who are working and selling products, the more the levels grow and the more money you make.

When I spoke to Pat Simecka, who with her husband, Don,

is now at the high rank of master coordinator after fifteen years with Shaklee, she told me about her serendipitous move into sales—and how, finally, she learned to use Shaklee's marketing plan to best advantage.

"I was a teacher and just couldn't imagine doing anything related to business, or, especially, sales," she said. "Then Don heard about Shaklee from a man he'd worked with who was retiring and looking for something to do." After much convincing Pat went to a Shaklee meeting, and still unsure, signed up.

"I didn't start out like a racehorse, like some fast-trackers," she told me. "In fact, I didn't pay attention to what the business could do for us, and I didn't know how to do a lot of things to build it up. It took me almost two years to the date to make the first official rank in Shaklee. Back then, I thought all the money would be in retail sales, not in recruiting. Then at a meeting, someone held up charts and I took a good look at the numbers. What I had to do was recruit, and help others recruit, too. At that point, I had the determination, and a strong desire to create something that was mine, so I decided to go for it and commit myself to the business."

In Pat's first year, she earned about $6,800, less than what she'd made at her teaching job. By the end of the third year, focusing on recruiting, she earned $18,000. By then, Don joined her in the business and, between them, their income went up to $72,000 by the sixth year with Shaklee full-time.

Pat and Don work together, planning the strategies to help themselves reach their goals. "We want our recruits to build their businesses, and Don will assist them with that. I make calls, take care of the orders and product demonstrations, and motivate others. Don and I work together as a team and our people find strength in that."

How Don and Pat earn more money through recruiting and helping others achieve their secret of multilevel marketing, and it's simple to learn. Here's how it works—with all its possibilities:

NOTE: The diagrams on the following pages represent a **theoretical** situation with a company. This is **not** any one company's marketing plan, but it is merely to show you how you can earn more money in direct sales. **Keep in mind that different companies operate differently in terms of how they handle their product distribution**—Amway and Shaklee salespeople order products (for their own use as well as for their retail customers) through their sponsors, who get a commission on all sales. On the other hand, Discovery Toys, Mary Kay, and Natural Impressions salespeople order their products at wholesale directly from the company with no intermediary.

Now, let me explain how some companies' plans work.

A friend recruits you and you build retail sales, increasing your income with each new customer. Suppose, now, that you have 20 customers. To simplify things, let's assume one circle represents your 20 customers. Your business will now look like this:

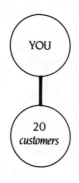

Diagram 1

The company's policy may be a 50 percent discount on inventory ordered directly from them in certain quantities with a suggested retail price. For our example here, let's use a retail price of 50 percent of retail. If each of your 20 customers buys $100 worth of products, you'll take in $2,000. One half of that pays for inventory, so you'll earn $1,000 gross profit.

Suppose three of your customers, Pam, Tina, and Marge, decide to do what you do and want to be *recruited*. By sponsoring them, you may be eligible to move into the first level of bigger financial opportunity.

Each sales company will, in its marketing plan, let you know how many recruits you must have before you can claim a commission on recruits' sales. Let's assume this fictitious company considers you "first level" when you've got three recruits. Pictorially, your business will look like this:

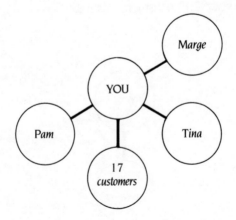

Diagram 2

Now that you've recruited Pam, Tina, and Marge, they'll buy their inventory directly from the company—instead of from you—but you'll now get a percentage from their sales. This percentage is called an "override" by some direct sales companies, "bonus commissions" by others. Either way the override is paid directly to you from the company and is *not* deducted from the new recruits' profits.

Pam, Tina, and Marge are now in business and each orders $1,000 in inventory for the retail customers they've found. Since these three recruits are all in your first level down, the company will pay you a first-level percentage—for example, 4 percent. Therefore, you'd earn $40 from each woman's effort (4 percent of $1,000) for a total sum of $120.

It doesn't stop here. Pam finds an eager customer to sponsor into the company from among her customers—Joan. Diagrammatically, the picture's getting much broader as your

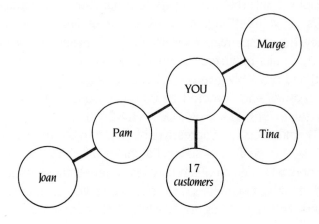

Diagram 3

income-producing possibilities grow (see Diagram 3). Joan is now in your *second* level, and you will earn a second-level commission from her sales.

You earn override commissions from Pam, Marge, and Tina customers (your first level), which will be different than the commission percentage from Joan, as your second level. If Joan recruits from among *her* customers, you'll be earning a commission percentage, too, on the *third* level. Again, the number of levels at which you can earn commissions and at what percentages depends on the individual company. Every company will establish its own percentage scale, which usually depends on the number of recruits you have and the dollar volume in sales.

As it stands now, you've personally recruited three people. Among them, only Pam has recruited one person (Joan) who may decide to sponsor others. Meanwhile, you still have your original 17 customers to sell products and to tap for recruiting. Suppose you *do* motivate two more customers to sign up (Toby, Nan). That now brings your number of personal recruits to five (see Diagram 4). Again, depending on payment policy, the company can reward you for bringing in *more* personal recruits by increasing your commission (say, to 8 percent) and probably give you a bonus or a gift. So . . . if your five recruits each ordered $1,000 in products one month, you'd earn $1,000 × 5 = $5,000 × 8% = $400.

The numbers are impressive, but it isn't quite this simple. We have to face the possibility that things will change and that numbers will fluctuate. Pam may lose some enthusiasm after a few months and be happy to coast along with her retail customers and not recruit for a while. Her recruit, Joan, who started out hesitantly, is now more confident and ambitious than Pam and outreaches her, bringing in two new recruits of her own, Nora and Lana. Of them, Lana starts out doing $300

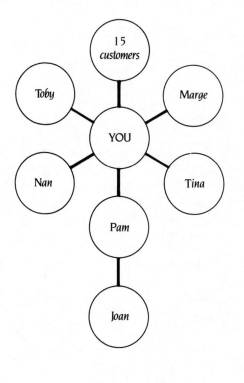

Diagram 4

a month in business for a few months, then, because of family problems, drops out. Joan, being conscientious, replaces her with Dina, who wants to pull together a dynamic organization of retail customers and motivated recruits.

How will you do financially?

You're drawing income from your own retail base of customers, commissions from your five recruits and two levels of their recruits. Things look better yet when Tina and Nan, in your organization, devote more time to business and each recruits three people. (see Diagram 5).

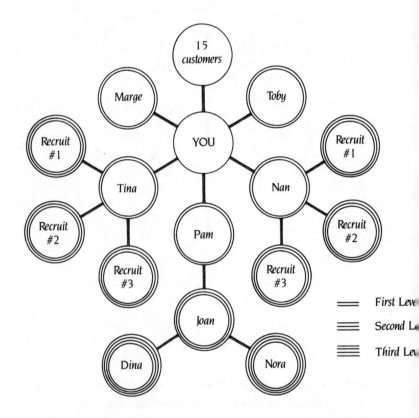

First Leve

Second L

Third Le

Diagram 5

Suppose Toby, Nan, Marge, Tina, and Pam are selling about $400 a month in products, while Nora, Joan, and Dina do about $300 each. Nan and Tina's three recruits, each new to the game, are doing $200 a month in business. You have 14 people selling, each with her own list of customers.

Your organization has generated $4,100 in sales. Your personal commission on a sum this high may be higher—let's say 13 percent. That totals $533. You'll also add to that the 50% profit on your own $400 in sales to retail customers, equaling $200. Your monthly earnings: $733.

		YOU			
Pam	Toby	Tina	Marge	Nan	1st level
Joan	Tina's 3 recruits		Nan's 3 recruits		2nd level
Nora	Dina				3rd level

Levels are sometimes called "generations." Your personal recruits are first generation; the second level is the second generation, or "grandchildren"; the third level contains your "great-grandchildren"; and so on for the fourth and fifth levels (when they are included in a company's marketing plan). You can, of course, keep recruiting people into your *first* level— bringing in as many as you can to effectively keep and motivate you. The number is unrestricted. This is what's meant by *lateral* growth—an ongoing process of personally recruiting people into your first level.

Pay Yourself What You're Worth

In terms of income, you receive overrides from several lines *down*ward, though it varies from company to company, depending on structure. In some companies, commissions vary because of the amount of inventory you order or, in others because of the level you are at in the company. In our example, the company is paying down *three* levels, then stops for "You." Let's see what will happen now.

Everyone in your organization has a turn at having a first through fifth level, since the format of direct sales plans is quite democratic. It works this way:

Pam (your recruit) is your *first* level and Joan (her recruit) is your *second*, and Dina is your *third*, but for Pam, Joan is *her* first level and Dina, her second and so on down. Since percentages on overrides usually change per level, you will want to help your recruits to recruit and sell to others.

Let's see what happens next:

Now that you have all these recruits who are building their organizations, you'll be earning percentages of their sales profits. At this point the company you work for may honor you with a title change and higher commission scale. You may become eligible for a bonus—cash, furs, jewelry, even a car. You'll be called a "director," or "coordinator," or something similar. The more your recruits earn, sell, and recruit people in turn, the greater your title.

Your commission percentage increases, too, and is usually determined, along with the title, by personal sales volume and the number of recruits personally sponsored within a certain amount of time.

About now, you'll discover another reason to keep recruiting and to build a large organization—one of your original recruits may "spin off" or become an "offspring" salesperson like you, taking the organization below them with them. But you haven't lost anyone at all. The typical company gives you a percentage of "offspring" commissions—about 4 or 5 percent on total volume. To illustrate: Pam has a change of heart and applies herself. She grows until she has five recruits of her own, who each have three of their own who've sponsored two recruits of their own. Pam's earning her company's specified minimum for the number of people in her organization over a period of time and can leave your direct circle—"spin off." If Pam's recruits have, between them, a few hundred customers, you can earn a nice sum just on that 4 or 5 percent.

Your organization will run smoothly after a while. You will become accustomed to the process of building retail customers and adding recruits when you can. You'll also discover the importance of teaching others what you know about sales techniques as well as sharing ideas about how to approach others. You'll be called upon to support others who falter or lose confidence—just as a good part of *your* early introduction to the business will be by attending meetings and staying in touch with others *to keep motivated*.

I must emphasize this: A generous exchange between novices and those experienced in direct sales can be responsible for *mutual* success. Kim St. Claire, who had a meteoric rise to the very top level of District Director with Jafra Cosmetics, enthusiastically agrees.

"When I started out, I read the guidebooks and did my best to make a sale," she told me from her home in Springfield, Massachusetts, "but I didn't have the big picture. Suddenly, after a year, it clicked. If I was to be a leader, I needed to help others get what they wanted, too. I asked myself, *what did they want*? I discovered that there were lots of women who were being paid what *others* thought they were worth and getting stuck there. I knew what that was like in my own life. I decided to do something about it."

Kim had been an office manager who "dabbled in" selling

Jafra products before she quit and devoted herself fully to a sales career. When she realized how encouraging, motivating, and teaching others could also enrich *her*, she connected to the very basis of direct sales. "I love watching people flourish as they develop self-confidence with each success. You can learn only so much from the guidebooks. I think everyone in sales needs support, needs to feel they are recognized, and to belong somewhere. With Jafra, I've gotten the kind of support that is more than business, it's *loving*. That's what makes people grow."

Kim, who is thirty-one years old, has been with Jafra since 1980. She's always shown a remarkable gift for the business. In her first year, she went through the motions and learned what she could in a practical way. She earned about $8,000. Once "things clicked," everything changed—in her second year, she earned $25,000. From there, her career was on a steady climb. She still holds the company record for sales and recruiting for a twelve-month period, she's the youngest of the four Fourth-Level District Directors (the top slot), *and* she's made it there in the shortest amount of time!

When you have developed a firm understanding of the business after a year or so and how you can work within the business, you can design a five-year plan of action to help you focus your effort to reach projected income goals. If you follow the plan, after eight or ten years you can earn major commission benefits from businesses you helped start to flourish years ago—companies that sprouted from companies that began with you.

Companies that work on commission *only* or commission *plus* bonuses for referrals and sales volume (Fuller Brush, Tupperware, for two), provide opportunities for excellent careers and feelings of accomplishment, though the ambitious salesperson will usually earn more money in the types of marketing plans described. The type of company you eventually choose doesn't matter as much as your commitment to it!

Let's take a closer look at sales—the actual selling situation—and see what really happens when a sale is made.

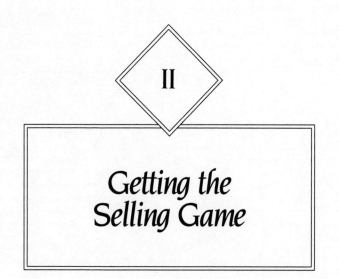

II

Getting the Selling Game

3

The Selling Game

When I first started out with Mary Kay Cosmetics, I didn't quite connect with the business of direct selling. I loved Mary Kay's products, used them, and freely recommended them to others, but what then? I had, after all, signed up for a career in sales, and to prove it, I had to transact business. So, I sold—actually called five or six people up, arranged for a skin care class, demonstrated the products for them, and took money in exchange for orders placed. This qualified me as a professional saleswoman, but I didn't feel like a saleswoman.

A *saleswoman*? The Mary Kay company officially designated us beginners as "beauty consultants"—which glamorized the position just enough. But I was a saleswoman, with kits, catalogs, and inventory to prove it. The sales *persona* made me a bit uncomfortable, and I had yet to sell one mascara or recruit a single person.

A part of that discomfort, I later realized, originated from a misunderstanding of what direct sales really was. I mistakenly thought of it entirely as a matter of persuasion. It could be coy or aggressive, but whatever the style, it was still one person with profit in mind persuading another person that he or she wanted what was being sold whether or not it was wanted. Would this be me?

The Mary Kay guidebooks (and her own autobiography) spoke of a company philosophy that was totally positive in tone. She stressed that we transact business by the golden rule—"Do unto others . . ." The book emphasized that success in sales wasn't achieved by pushing, but by drawing others out. I soon discovered that a number of other direct sales companies, too, agreed on a definition of sales that made perfect sense: Sales is simply **finding out what people want, then helping them get it by providing a service or fulfilling a need.** But I hadn't quite taken that definition to heart and made it a part of me.

And I shared some common opinions about the direct salesperson who might appear at the door. The image was less than admirable. A few words that came to mind were "aggressive," and "double-talker." I was also reminded of the character of Moses Pray, the charming hustler-of-a-salesman in the movie *Paper Moon*, who didn't think twice about deceiving poor widows and tricking them into buying Bibles. Bibles! So even though I fantasized about creating a dynamic career in sales, I began with a somewhat tarnished image of what a salesperson is commonly thought to be.

My first Mary Kay beauty show—or "skin care class"—was attended by my daughter Elizabeth and seven of her college friends—all of whom pretty much humored me for the occasion. Elizabeth was fairly unsure of what I was doing. It was my choosing *sales* that bothered her, not that I chose Mary Kay Cosmetics. To her, a sales career was a "rinky-dink" business not worthy of my time. She saw me as a talk show hostess, not someone toting a box of cosmetics, and driving a pink car. In her way, she reflected what others were thinking—that my entry into Mary Kay bespoke of upcoming personal calamity and eventual besmirching of the family name. As I mentioned earlier, you've got a 70–80 percent chance that those you love may not understand what you are doing and think your career choice a joke. The end result is that you not only have to battle through your own doubts, but at the same time, forge through *their* convictions that you're going to humiliate yourself, and them, at the same time. All these emotional encounters may not be easy at first, but they certainly can be handled successfully.

I decided to be cheerful and do my best at the beauty show. Everyone seemed to have a good time—and everyone bought our five basic skin care items. After the class was over, Elizabeth—who years later began pursuing her own career with Mary Kay—was a bit more convinced that I'd do okay, but not entirely. This skin care class was my maiden voyage, and though I enjoyed it immensely, secretly I still fretted over the image of "salesperson."

Then I organized my second beauty show and ran into some trouble. At the end of the evening, I came up with zero—not one sale. Was this the business for me? I still loved the products, but now I doubted if enthusiasm for the products was enough. I made more phone calls and was rejected. I can remember more than one time I was even insulted, when a polite no would have made the point. Before joining the company, I was great at recommending Mary Kay products to others, who subsequently went off and bought them from other beauty consultants. My sister-in-law, for one. Ironically, she had just bought the whole Mary Kay line the day before I called her. She told me that it was because I'd been raving about the products for so long that decided it for her—and she didn't know I'd gone ahead and signed up with the company! She'd even agreed to invite friends in for a demonstration show in her home the following week. Another rejection, and one I didn't expect, came from a friend of mine who was the wife of one of the Minnesota Vikings, whose answer to my offer of a complimentary facial was "Uck!" Then I called an old friend who said, "You haven't called me in eight years! Why are you calling now?" I told her, and she signed up! Finally, a success. My career was growing very slowly, but I was learning about people and getting stronger at dealing with rejection. I decided to call the wives of the Vikings' coaches, and this time, had a very successful show, which helped to eventually launch my career. Two weeks had passed.

Not one to give up, I set up a fourth class, then a fifth, and while driving to the sixth class, I had a revelation. My strong suits were energy and enthusiasm. My weak suit was worrying about what others thought about me. I suddenly realized that by giving in to this feeling, I was ignoring what sales really meant. I was letting these worries accompany me to beauty shows and influence me negatively more than I'd suspected. The fact was that I had nothing to be ashamed of! I represented a company that was founded on fine principles and that produced a superior product and offered excellent career opportunities.

I'd lost sight of my original goal: to succeed by being the best I could be. I was interested in phasing out my TV career after a seven-year run and now I wanted to turn my skills to business.

People often remark on my shift from glamorous TV hostess to Mary Kay representative, believing the sales career to be a downshift from the TV job. Hosting a show *did* have glamour, but my earning potential at the station was very limited. A few other problems existed, too: I wasn't allowed to make many decisions there, the atmosphere on the show could be strained, and sometimes, sadly, management forgot to acknowledge our staff's contributions to high ratings.

Once I knew for sure that I'd be leaving TV, I took advantage of the hours outside the few each day I spent on the set, and used the extra time to build my career with Mary Kay. I "overlapped" both careers for two-and-a-half years, and was able to make a stunning comparison between them. Unlike my experience in my TV job, I was praised from my very first success in sales, and I continued to get praise from Mary Kay Ash—by phone, by letter, and in person—on my way to the top. This kind of personal acknowledgment was, and always will be, most important to me. Praise was surely missing for me in TV, but it was in *abundance* in direct sales.

When I left the station at last to work full-time in sales, I reminded myself over and over again of the following:

- ◆ Sales was my career and I was going to show up for it—prepared and enthusiastic.

- ◆ Sales was my career now and I wouldn't let others decide my fate, as I had had to with a salaried job.

- ◆ Sales was my career and I was going to give it everything I had, make it work, and be proud of it!

As I see it, the one quality that has been and will always be the measure of success—for me or for anyone else—is *a good attitude*. Without it, we focus on the setbacks, flops, and mistakes, letting our disappointments shape our lives. Without a good attitude, we concentrate on rejections rather than meet challenges and attain goals.

When I started out, I did a few "wrongs." For example, I appeared at a skin care class only to discover that I'd forgotten to bring along some essentials, like demonstration trays or flip charts. (Believe me, they're necessary!) It could have been easy to concentrate on the goof-up, get all shook up about forgetting something, and overdo on apologies, but where would such a negative attitude have gotten me? Nowhere. And no one would have felt comfortable with the selling situation if I had brought my error to their attention.

Instead, I improvised when I needed to (substituting paper plates, for example, for demonstration trays), focused on the point of the evening, and eased right into doing the best I could under the circumstances. Letter-perfect presentations don't necessarily win the sale or guarantee a successful career unless you go in there with heart, a sense of humor, and a little grace under pressure. I'm one example of someone who is resourceful and positive when I've gotten some of the details wrong.

I suppose all of us in sales would describe what we get out of sales in different terms, but everyone would agree: **You can do everything wrong with the right attitude and succeed and do everything right with the wrong attitude and fail!**

So, to backtrack a minute: Personality *does* count, but it's not enough. One woman can zealously sell herself and incidentally sell the product and service. She's one type of salesperson who foils her career in spite of herself. Another self-defeating type may focus on the product, and barrage the retail or wholesale customer with statistics, testimonials, and sources for further information. Yet a third may decide that the most important sales point is to sell the career and recruit anyone by emphasizing claims for income earned within a short period of time.

The route to success in this business is, then, beginning with a good attitude, then simply finding the balance between:

♦ selling *yourself* (enthusiastic, honest, well groomed)

♦ selling the *product* (superior or unusual in some way; guaranteed)

♦ selling your *service* (convenience, personal touch of buying direct)

♦ selling the *company* (reputable, well run)

♦ selling the *career* (offers opportunity and growth)

Anything you say or do during a meeting with a potential customer involves a little of each of these points. There will be a shift in emphasis as it's called for: you may demonstrate a product, for example, but needn't stress its ingredients as the reason to buy it. Your customer wants to be told how it will improve his/her life and/or looks, first of all. And if you're recruiting, you're not only selling products, you're setting an example while describing the benefits of a career with the company you represent. At the end of the meeting, if you make a sale or sign a recruit, you've done your job.

You needn't have the company presentation memorized to the last suggested inflection to be a top salesperson. You needn't know everything about the industry or carry hand-written testimonials from satisfied customers. Success in direct sales depends on understanding people, their behavior, and their motives for buying. It's about approach and positive reinforcement, all the while remembering this important definition of sales: **Find out what people want, then help them get it by providing a service or filling a need.**

"If you feel you're performing a service," said Beverly Worthing, a Fuller Brush representative in Chandler, Arizona, "sales will work differently for you than if you think you must only concentrate on the numbers."

Beverly manages a psychiatrist's office by day, and to fill some extra time since her husband works nights, Beverly became a direct salesperson. That was three years ago. She's had some high and low points, but feels very optimistic. "I like the idea of selling—the more I sell, the more I increase my confidence. I love the products, the people I meet, and the opportunities it can bring."

This concept—discovering the need and providing the service—begins any selling process. It's the perfect guide to steer you to your goal.

Since most direct sales transactions start with contact by phone, let's open there. We'll imagine you, at home, with pen and pad and the phone numbers of potential customers or recruits.

First Contact: Making Calls and Appointments

The Phone Is Your Friend

The novice salesperson may think of contact calls and blind dates with an equal amount of emotional upheaval. First she worries about getting the names of people to call, then, after calling, she wants to give up in despair when one or two don't work out. Too many and too high expectations are classic impediments to making the third, fourth . . . hundredth call. So shrug off the disappointments. They happen to everyone who is in business and uses the phone as a selling tool. Art Nielsen (whose company is the A. C. Nielsen television rating service) once told me the story of working with his father when they began their business. Everyone told them, as they made their calls, that a television rating service "won't work." Then, as they approached the end of an unsuccessful afternoon, Art, Jr. wanted to give up and quit for the day. His father still said excitedly, "But Artie, we have time for *one more* call." *That* was the fateful call that launched the enormously successful and now legendary "Nielsen Ratings."

Everyone knows at least thirty people—relatives, friends of relatives, shopkeepers, teachers, and so on. Call them and ask for referrals. Keep at it! Make that call no matter how weighty the phone feels in your hand. You're in the direct sales business. You need to sell person-to-person, and to sell you must make appointments. Learn to use the phone to your advantage, and you'll see it's not as tough as you may think.

Your best bet for success is to establish a routine and follow a plan of action. Begin with . . .

Objectives

Keep business in mind. You're not calling to chat, pass time, or gossip. These familiar forms of interaction are for socializing only. The reason you're making the call is to get an appointment with a prospect and eventually to make a sale.

Before even dialing the number, make a note of the two basic objectives you'll want to accomplish by the end of the call:

1) *to make contact only with the actual person who'll be doing the purchasing.* Your objective is to get to the *right* person or to find out when the best time is to reach him or her. When you're calling the person at home, you don't want to waste time explaining your business in detail to a spouse, child, baby-sitter, relative, or friend who happens to answer the phone instead. Don't ask them if your contact would be interested in your product or service. Leave your name and number and if they don't return the call, try again. If you're contacting prospects at the office, and they cannot get to the phone, leave your

name and ask when they'll be available to speak to you. Then call back.

2) *to set up an appointment.* You cannot really make a sale over the phone in a very limited amount of time, because you need to demonstrate and explain the benefits of your product in person. Therefore, your objective is to *get in* to see the prospect before you can make the sale. Keep your calendar ready for when you get the appointment.

Early on in the game, many salespeople chatter on nervously after making the appointment. Perhaps we're feeling unsure of ourselves at the moment, and so we begin to reiterate portions of the sales talk just to be safe! I've done this myself—rattling on, *re*selling a woman on the career, the products, how she'll enjoy seminars in Dallas, and on and on. This does not help the sale or set a good example.

Stop talking once you've made the appointment. Be excited about the upcoming meeting with your prospect, then end the call right there.

Objectives established. You'll now want to clarify what it is you're going to say in what amount of time and to whom. These are . . .

Precall Imperatives

♦ ***Set up a quiet environment.*** There will always be some noisy disturbances beyond your control like an army of electric company drill press operators tearing up your street midway into your call. But, in general, it's up to you to phone a prospect only when there is nothing but silence or very low, undistracting sounds around you. Nothing dampens your professional credibility as much as having to shout over a loud TV or screaming children.

◆ **Know a little about your prospect.** You most likely got his or her name from someone who knew someone. Try to fill out a biography to match the name. This would include general information about income, tastes, family status, possible needs your product can fill. The more you know about a prospect, the more you can anticipate objections to buying, and overcome them.

◆ **Write a script.** If you're a genius at improvisation and can reel off the details of your selling speech like a virtuoso, go to it. Most of us do better in the beginning when we write down what we want to say, then rehearse it till it sounds smooth, professional, and *un*rehearsed. Scripting and practicing the script gives you greater confidence each time you make a call.

You may get to a point where you know the script but still feel "stage fright." In that case, ask an ally to give you that final push to make the call. Marilyn Welle's story is a good example of this:

When I was still on television, Marilyn, the woman who recruited me, was herself fairly new to sales. Once she decided to contact me, she rehearsed her script for her family to get it letter-perfect before the actual phone call. Marilyn's six children heard the script so often, they could mouth the words along with her. The problem with her was talking the script to *me*. She'd pick up the phone, call, and would be relieved when I wasn't in. Marilyn told me all she could think about was rejection. One day, her children challenged her fear and asked the right questions: "What's the worse thing that could happen to you? That Shirley will say no?"

Marilyn saw the point: If I rejected her, she was still a good person who knew her business; she could just go on to the next prospect. So, she made the call to me, did her script as smoothly as she had a hundred times before for her children, and, to her surprise, the script worked. I said yes.

◆ *Be prepared for a short phone call.* Nearly all direct sales companies suggest that their salespeople limit business phone calls to three minutes. This is enough time for amenities and setting up a meeting without a sense of rushing off the phone. Busy people who don't have three minutes, but have just half a minute to listen will tell you so. If you open a call with the statement, "I'd like to talk to you about a great business opportunity. Do you have a minute?" *listen to the answer.* Don't sell them on an appointment by speed-speaking your script in thirty seconds, or leaving out crucial details because of the time limit. You will *not* sound professional—just frantic or desperate for a sale. Neither should you figure that if you've only got half a minute, you may as well finish it off with useless social chatter. Novice salespeople have done this with me: I may only have a minute because I'm rushing off to the airport, tell them so, and they go on about how *they* missed a plane because of roadblocks or terrible weather! They think they're personalizing the call and making me feel better, but I'd rather have just gotten their name and called back when I had time. Remember: The person with thirty seconds to spare wasn't waiting for your call to relax with weather reports. Don't entertain him/her. Use the thirty seconds to *make an appointment.* If you've got more time, the prospect will keep speaking to you without mentioning time limits. Most speeches can be honed down to 180 seconds and still have impact. Practice.

◆ *Don't be put off by coolness or negativity.* This reaction can be rough for most of us because it can mean rejection. An irritated or angry voice on the other end brings up that queasy feeling below the heart. Don't take it personally. Instead, take a deep breath and be pleasant. Unless you're personally insulted beyond the purpose of the call, be understanding of their momentary agitation and offer to call back. You may have gotten them right after a fight with a spouse or the plumber; unpleasant news might have reached them right before your call. Allow for unpredictable responses and bad moods on the other end.

Rejection isn't fun, but it's part of the selling game. A *Psychology Today* article on sales, written by Donald J. Moine, commented so accurately: "Sales, perhaps more than any other profession, is a psychological laboratory for testing human intelligence, persistence, persuasiveness, and resilience: the ability to deal with rejection on a daily basis."

It may surprise you to learn that successful salespeople feel rejection, but they don't let it direct their lives. Just chalk up a no, remember it's their loss, give yourself points for trying, and *dial the next number*.

Making the call

◆ **Identify yourself and why you're calling.** Lead in with your name, company affiliation, and who referred you, if that's the case. You automatically become a little more than an unfamiliar voice on the phone: "Betty, this is Jane Green. Barbara Bennett suggested I call you. I'm a sales director with Mary Kay Cosmetics and I'd like to set up an appointment with you for a complimentary facial. Do you have a minute to talk?"

If you can establish a "grabber"—a benefit for them—do it in the introduction. In this case I offered her a complimentary facial. With other companies, you could mention a free gift (Fuller Brush), or stress convenience and custom styling (Doncaster) or suggest quality in health products bought wholesale (Shaklee). Since they don't have the product in front of them to touch, see, smell, or taste, you're arousing their interest with more of a reason to keep listening, even if it's just information they can use.

Let's assume Betty takes the call and doesn't put you off. Bring up a personal but safe bit of information you've learned about her from your contact. Take the next sales step: "Barbara told me you're such a busy person these days, but I'd like the opportunity to have you try our products. There's no obligation to you, Betty. And I know you'll love them."

You've acknowledged her schedule and hopefully drawn her psychologically into the selling process. She knows it will cost her nothing to try the products (or examine the samples), besides getting a token gift for her time. Depending on the company, you may want to stress the convenience of direct sales or the kind of needed service you'll provide.

◆ *Make the appointment for her.* Betty is still interested and on the phone; you're enthusiastic. Tell her *when* you'd like to demonstrate the products or show the new line. Do not ask her *if* she's got the time. "I'm having a skin care class this coming Monday, and I'd love to include you. The class is limited to six, though, so I should make a reservation for you now."

The skin care class for Mary Kay products is a variation of the "party plan," popularized by Tupperware and Stanley Home Products (Stanhome). Jafra, Sarah Coventry, and Shaklee are three other companies (among others) who also use this selling technique. If your company's policy recommends one-to-one selling, make the appointment with: "I'll be happy to come over Monday or Tuesday afternoon of next week. I know you're busy and so am I, but I'll juggle my schedule to what's best for you." Then, if she cannot attend, ask her,

"Which is better for you? Morning, afternoon, or evening; the beginning or end of the week?"

While she's deciding, reinforce a selling point: "I'm looking forward to meeting you, Betty. Barbara told me you'd been thinking about trying our products. I know you'll be really pleased when you do."

◆ *Get the appointment.* If Betty can't make it Monday (party plan) or either day (one-to-one), keep negotiating until you both set an absolute date and time. My recommendation is to never book more than two weeks ahead—people cancel out more freely. In the case of party plan, I'd go to see Betty personally if it looked as if she could *not* get to a skin care class for a month or so. I don't want to lose her as a potential customer or recruit, and I'll see her at *any* time that doesn't conflict with another appointment and is convenient for her.

Reminders

- Keep the call warm and interactive. Use the name of the person who recommended her as well as the prospect's name in the conversation. This will draw her into the selling process.

- State the benefit or service your product offers.

- Use compliments without gushing.

- Don't sell the products over the phone, but sell yourself.

- Tantalize the prospect to get an appointment.

- Make the appointment!

But What If Betty Says No

Betty may bring up objections in response to your introduction: she's too busy . . . she's loyal to a product not unlike the one you're selling and sees no reason to switch . . . she's low on cash right now. Regard her objections one at a time:

♦ **She's too busy.** If you cannot get her to make a tentative appointment, strongly recommend the product to her and ask once more for a meeting: "Betty, using these products will bring you compliments! I'd love the chance to have you try them. I can call again in three weeks and see how your schedule is." Don't stop talking until you get a firm NO! Betty may be unable to say no and will come back with: "I'm just not interested." At this juncture, I'd be direct and ask her: "Is there any season that might be a better time to meet with you? Or, is it that you don't want to try the products at all?" If she says it's okay to call sometime in the future, thank her and end on a warm note. Should she decline, thank her and leave with a pleasant "I'll be thinking of you, Betty, and hope we can meet someday." *Immediately, make your next call.*

♦ **She's loyal to another product.** Agree with her on her choice, then segue to your proposal: "I know, Betty, the ABC Makeup Company markets a wonderful product. That's why I'd like your opinion of Mary Kay's." Betty's still loyal to the ABC Company and won't back down to book an appointment. You may have to end with: "Betty, use the ABC products for now, but I'm going to be thinking of you and call back. In the meantime, can you think of someone who would enjoy a complimentary facial? Perhaps you have a friend who isn't as happy as she could be with the products she's using, or a friend with skin problems, or just someone you'd like to do something nice for? If so, I'd like to have her name, and, for the referral, I'll have a lovely gift for you."

If you don't get a chance for a sale with Betty, be courageous and ask for a referral. There's nothing to lose at this point.

When your product is clothing, make an effort to find out if Betty's loyalty is directed at prestige designer labels or economy lines. Sell her on your company's service, the detailing, the fabric, the understated look at the right price, the fashion sense: "If you want a designer label, I can't help you, Betty. But I can offer the kind of value and personal service you won't find in a store for a comparable price." Are you selling housewares, jewelry, fragrances, books, products that "go down the drain"—shampoo, detergents, cleaning fluids, etc.—vitamins or health foods? Emphasize what makes your product *different* and of *greater value* and *benefit* to her. Again, if she refuses, suggest calling her again in six months.

♦ *She's low on cash.* Most direct sales companies have low starter fees, no starter fees, or a minimal amount to stock a sample case or demonstration kit. This might be a good opportunity to ask if she's interested in trying your product at no cost to her with the idea of joining your company. Get more information from her. Be sensitive to the situation. Probe without her feeling that you're intruding into her life or suggesting a course of action that might offend her: "Betty, I *understand.* So many people in direct sales have created terrific careers starting out with your exact problem! I'd like to drop by to show you the range of products and have you try them. I can also bring information about the company and show you how easy and low-cost it would be for you to begin a part-time or full-time career with us."

If she's interested in hearing more, relate one example of a success story that she can identify with. Then try to get an appointment. Don't stop until you get a firm NO!

Final Reminders On Calling

It'll take a bit of experience, but you'll soon master the art of telephone techniques. Once again, I can guarantee greater success if you approach the whole matter with a positive atti-tude. Your prospects will be able to discern boredom or leth-argy or irritation in your tone of voice. If *you* project indifference, why should *they* be enthusiastic and buy?

Psychiatrist David Viscott, M.D., in his book *Taking Care of Business*, listed what messages a voice should convey to others on a business call. They are:

- ◆ "I'm glad you called."

- ◆ "I have the time to understand what you want."

- ◆ "We can solve it."

- ◆ "I'm sure we can find a way to work together."

- ◆ "You matter."

- ◆ "Your business is important."

- ◆ "This is a good place to work."

- ◆ "We like people."

Making the Sale: Prepare Yourself, Be Aware of Yourself

Enthusiasm

Anyone who is successful in direct sales knows how important the right attitude is in this business, and that begins with enthusiasm. Without it, we're pretty much nowhere. I can't imagine selling a product by droning on noncommittally about it or describing a job to someone in an offhand or dejected manner and hope they are inspired to do what I do!

At a meeting I attended a number of years ago, a Mary Kay national sales director revealed an interesting side of herself. She told us this story. Sometimes, she's feeling low or exhausted, but it's Sunday night and she's got to make phone calls to gather people for her Monday meetings. She's not interested in turning the focus of the call onto herself and why she might be worn out. Instead, she wants to get everyone fired up to do business that will take place twenty-four hours from then. So, if she's out of natural enthusiasm, she fakes it by running up and down her stairs a few times! When she's nearly breathless, she dashes to the phone, dials a number, and says in what passes for (nearly breathless) *genuine* enthusiasm in her voice, "Oh, Jane! I can't wait to tell you about our meeting tomorrow and I want you to please come as my guest!" The trick works for her and has helped her become one of the top people in the company.

Though we need a solid foundation of information and expertise—which we eventually acquire through experience—it's enthusiasm that gets us, if not breathless, then *eager* and committed. Enthusiasm, I truly believe, is not only important, but it's often the make-or-break factor in a sale. Without that injection of personal energy, sales would be a dreary, mechanical act much like dropping a coin in a vending machine, pulling the lever, and fishing the candy out of the slot.

Enthusiasm is **motivating**. It creates a sense of activity. One sale gets you going. You want to duplicate that success and keep selling!

Enthusiasm is **seductive**—all that bounce, excitement, and *hope*.

Enthusiasm is **contagious**. When you love what you sell, others may not only buy from you, but some will be inspired enough to join your business and thereby (in a number of cases) increase your income.

Enthusiasm is **critical to success** in sales, but it requires a solid foundation to support it. Unless there's commitment, responsibility, follow-through, it's impossible to build an ongoing career.

Enthusiasm can also **spark original ideas**. Even a miracle can happen, as with a $35,000 commission on a sale made in the course of an hour or so. It happened this way:

One morning when I was driving past the bank, I got a flash that a bank might be a good place to sell Mary Kay products—but in a unique way. The bank was one of those multiservice operations that offered premiums—gifts, really—to new depositors who opened a savings account and were obliged to leave the money in for a prescribed period of time. At some point or other, you've probably opened such an account, and gotten a choice of heating pad, electric fry pan, blanket, or any one of the usual assortment of housewares. So had I. Then I thought, why not investigate the bank's policy of adding cosmetics to the promotion? I called and made an appointment to see a manager there.

I'd only been selling about a year on a part-time basis when I set up this meeting. My selling point to the bank was that not only were the products terrific, but they were an unusual premium that would gain attention and draw a greater number of depositors. So, determined to do the seemingly impossible, I covered the manager's desk with samples, and proceeded to demonstrate them. He tried the lotions and fragrances on his wrist while any female bank employee who chanced to walk by and look into his office was invited to try anything she chose. Everyone appeared pleased.

And so . . . about an hour later, I left with a huge order from the bank. They were as sure as I was that the Mary Kay line would be right for them.

Months later, I asked the manager why he chose to buy my line of products. He told me that salespeople come and sit in his office and drone on about their products—clocks, blankets, whatever. No matter what they're selling me, he said, they sound *bored*. "You were so enthusiastic," he told me, "I was sold immediately."

I couldn't tell you what was in my actual sales presentation and I'm sure that he couldn't either. Actually, it didn't matter. I know that my presentation and product demonstration may have had clumsy moments, but it was fulfilling to know that genuine enthusiasm tipped the scales toward success.

Careers can find a basis in a positive attitude and amiability. But a sales career cannot be built solely on charm, though many a charmer has tried. Enthusiasm can actually be *misused* and interfere with progress and success.

To demonstrate, there's the true story of a onetime friend, whom I protect with the name Vicki—a woman believing entirely in the power of "sizzle" to advance her career.

Vicki thought she was born to sell—that she could talk anyone into buying anything. Her strong points were star-quality personality and magnetism, but you also believed in her. She showed sincere interest in *you*. She got you to need whatever she was selling in a way that fully convinced you it was *your* idea to invite her over so you could buy what she sold!

Unfortunately, Vicki was as charmed by her own dynamism as any of her captivated clients or customers. She liked perpetuating the image of the great sales personality— winning friends while clinching deals and making money. Her problem? Her "hustle" had a flip side that wasn't so endearing. Instead of seeing her sale through to the end, she would lose interest midway and chase off to sell the next guy!

Vicki would forget the details—like getting shipments on time, placing orders correctly, and following up. In the process, she irritated and inconvenienced people and consequently lost many sales.

Know that compelling personality may get you in the door (even win you a second or third chance to make good when you mess up), but it's wasted effort unless you remember the golden rule of sales: *No company can operate by only selling someone once.* And the best way to sell someone something once is to not deliver what was originally promised. Vicki was guilty of this.

Many businesses (large and small) have tumbled with a Vicki (or Vic) selling nothing but blue sky. And many careers have been sunk when a Vic (or a Vicki) tried to get by on personality alone while neglecting the actual details of running a business.

Just as people may be fooled by sizzle (but not too often from the same source), so will they *not* be taken in by false enthusiasm for very long. Phoniness shows. Almost everyone sees through the act. It puts a dreadful strain on you, and you may turn off your sales prospects forever.

The best you can do is to *like* your product and *love* selling it.

Body Language

Let's assume you're in sales and are facing two very different prospects. The first, Mr. Brown, is distracted and seems irritated. His forehead is wrinkled and his arms are crossed tightly on his chest. He's listening to you, and though he's not saying no, he's certainly not saying yes either.

The second man, Mr. Davis, is also there, sitting opposite you. He seems attentive and has a pleasant expression on his face. His hands are resting casually on the table. He's also not saying yes, but he's not saying no either.

Which of these two men would be your most likely customer? I'd choose the latter without a moment's hesitation.

Why? The second list of signals tells you immediately that you have a chance! First, the attentive attitude—Mr. Davis is with you. He seems to be listening to what you have to say. Mr. Brown is not interested and it seems like he'd rather be doing something else. (Keep in mind that sometimes a distracted manner is just a way for the person to think he's in charge of the situation. He may want you to work harder to get his sale by making you think you'll be rejected at any moment. Experience will soon tell you if this is the case and if you've really lost the sale or if you should give your prospect a few extra minutes and a compliment.)

The second body language clue as to which person is easier to sell is that Mr. Davis appears to be pleased in your company. Some people can say no with a smile, but if they're listening to you with a pleasant expression while you're trying to make a sale, you probably will. Rarely will you hear a yes formed by pursed lips or "I'll take it," uttered through a frown. That easygoing look speaks *approval*. Mr. Brown is probably doubtful or disapproving about what he's hearing—to wit, his furrowed brow.

A third clue to what each man is thinking is his body language. Mr. Davis is not exactly touching you, but by extending his arms outward on the table in a relaxed way, he reveals he's comfortable with you and what you're doing. It's a welcoming gesture. And Mr. Brown? Arms crossed on the chest is both a self-protective gesture and one that keeps you at a distance. Arms crossed this way usually signifies disapproval at what's happening and may be accompanied by a negative remark.

Mr. Brown and Mr. Davis demonstrate the simpler forms of body language—those unspoken words and nonverbal clues that reveal additional information as to how they're feeling or thinking. Like Brown and Davis, everyone uses body language and uses it all the time. Sometimes it's done so unconsciously that you're not even aware of how you're sitting or what expression is on your face. I'm sure you have had people respond verbally to your *non*verbal opinions, and it's surprised you.

At various times, body language signals friends, foes, and family to come forward or stay away—to tell them we dislike or distrust them, that we love or feel fondly toward them. All this is revealed to us literally by the subtle blink of an eye, a slouch, or the tip of a head.

I include the science of body language because it's such a big part of selling. These subtle signals are critical helpmates in sales—tune in to them correctly and project positive ones of your own, and you'll increase sales success tenfold! Especially in direct sales. You're always one-on-one with a potential customer in a fairly intimate setting—that is, their house or a friend's house. They're in a cordial, familiar environment, and hopefully, more comfortable and more open to a sale. You not only bring your products with you, but you bring your goals and . . . your own body language. Are you like Mr. Brown or Mr. Davis when dealing with a potential customer?

Books have been written on body language—with full "dictionaries" to clarify the meaning of gestures. They're worth reading and, I think, you'll enjoy them as well for their entertaining aspect of self-recognition. At the very least, you should be aware of these few important body signals:

♦ Spoken words have a greater impact psychologically if they are said standing up while those listening are sitting. A similar benefit can be had if the authority is sitting on a taller chair or on a chair separated from the group to give the illusion of being superior. The superior/inferior position is common, for example, with teachers and students. This position lets others know that you're in command while imparting information.

♦ In sales, however, you're going to strive for a point closer to equality—letting others be slightly in the "superior" position without you actually feeling "inferior." I think this is the best bet for better communication: Sit *next to* your potential customers and lean in toward them. Dipping a bit automatically creates the sensation of being slightly submissive—even if you're pounds heavier and inches bigger than the customer.

♦ I know there is nothing more unsettling than being stared at for a long period of time. You feel as if you're being scrutinized. Salespeople are often reminded to maintain eye contact, but don't overdo it, as if you were a night club hypnotist instead of a friendly merchandiser. You may think it appears as if you're *fascinated*, but most folks find the stare intrusive—and challenging.

◆ Not making eye contact for more than a fragment of a second is equally straining. Most people don't trust anyone who won't look at them—as if they have something to hide. What you're hiding (or protecting) may be your self-consciousness and shyness, but it's read (in body language terms) as a *negative* sign. If you have trouble looking at someone for normal amounts of time, practice eye contact on yourself in the mirror.

◆ Leg swinging, leg shaking, pen clicking, or any other distracting habit or gesture only draws attention to you (and the tic) and away from your intention, which is to *make a sale*. Be aware of how you sit when speaking to others. I know you may be nervous the first few times out and in spite of yourself, some part of you may set itself in motion, like leg shaking. To help offset these sometimes unconscious tics, practice your speech out loud at home and rehearse what you want to say. Ask yourself the kind of challenging, nervous-making questions you think you might be asked by customers or recruits. *Feel* what happens to your system. If you simulate the experience and prepare yourself with answers to these questions, you'll definitely feel more relaxed when you get to the *real* thing. Preparation, experience, and rehearsal are often the cure for "the shakes."

Dressing Appropriately

Sleeveless blouses/slogan T-shirts/Hawaiian shirts/sweatshirts/scuffed shoes and run-down heels/loose or missing buttons/stained ties/ill-fitting pants or trousers/mismatched outfits/multiple-pierced ears with an assortment of dangling earrings—any accessory or item of clothing that demands attention is fine for any occasion you so choose except for one: when you're selling.

How you appear to others in the selling game will matter. Project a careless image in your dress and your prospects may not care to buy from you. Project a professional look and you'll establish credibility and trust.

You needn't overdress or overspend on wardrobe—just be aware of assembling a neutral, neat, and stylish look for every meeting. The company you work with may also offer guidelines—Mary Kay, for one, requests that women do not wear slacks when working. Get in the habit of looking good to yourself and others. This includes being in touch with the general economic level of your prospects, too. When you appear at a trailer court with your sample kit, recruits-to-be or customers can be intimidated if you look too prosperous. Relate to them: be casually tailored in nondistracting styling and fabrics. The reverse is true, of course, when you're selling to people in the upper end of the economic scale. Wear clothing that makes you look successful. And if you sell clothing, what could be better than to wear an item from your line that is flattering to you?

Two side notes: If you've won award pins, ribbons, or jewelry, try not to wear more than *one* at a time. I've seen some salespeople who go out in the field decorated with clusters of glittery pins given out for some sort of achievement—high sales figures, large numbers of recruits within a short amount of time, and so on. Decorations like these are distracting to customers. Better yet, don't wear any of them when you're out selling. Second, it's also a good idea for women to carry an extra pair of pantyhose with them and for men to take along an extra tie.

Making a Sale

As a salesperson, your purpose is to uncover the real reason people might want to buy your product. In direct selling, you also want the product to interest the person enough for him to want to sell it, too. How do we know what people will buy? How *do* customers make a decision?

"A man generally has two reasons for doing a thing—one that sounds good, and a real one." This axiom, attributed to the late banking genius, J. P. Morgan, is familiar to those of us in sales and is proved true repeatedly in the field. Why do people *buy* or why do they *pass you by*? The answer is found in how the product meets the individual needs of each person. Product "needs" fall into the following categories:

- ◆ The product enriches life, making it more comfortable.

- ◆ The product makes tasks easier or promotes efficiency.

- ◆ The product satisfies a need for status.

- ◆ The product makes someone feel good when it's used.

Successful salespeople are always keyed in to customers' needs, and many of them fulfill those needs in what they think of as "service." Duncan Christopher, a New York actor-choreographer and an Amway profit-sharing distributor for three years, says, "As I see it, we all tend to relate more to money, to transacting a sale. I believe in *service*. When I relate sales to service, it makes all the difference. If I meet some people who are resistant or doubtful or negative at first, I try to pass through their considerations and ask questions to see where they're coming from. I find out what they need and how I can serve them, and present things to them this way. I know people buy because they've decided to buy. My job is to help move them along to make that decision."

There's a definite wisdom in Duncan's thinking: no one likes to be pressed into buying what the salesperson is selling, but people like the feeling of being served. Customers may not even know what they need (or want) when you first begin your presentation, but that's okay. Or, a customer may want your product, even want it desperately, but if you push it too vigorously, she may back off and buy elsewhere. Remember, a sale is made in the mind of a customer first. *People buy because they decide to buy*. The right reason came up for them.

Barbara Hammond, now a vice president of Home Interiors, also promotes the concept of sales as service. "To succeed in sales," she told me, "you have to be in love with serving people. Building a career is truly loving to serve. You may be selling products, but you also wind up getting involved with customers, too, and you have to care."

Barbara, who has commuted monthly from her Fresno, California home to her Dallas-based office for fifteen of her twenty-six years with the company, specializes in training management and giving inspirational and motivational talks. "I think one big mistake salespeople make is in deciding they're *imposing* on customers—that is, imposing on them to buy or hold a show or be recruited. It's not an imposition, but a marvelous service that cannot be bought in a store. Once you accept the idea of service, it shades your outlook. You will tend to have a more positive, giving outlook. To me, then, the winning combination is finding the company you respect that makes a product you can relate to, falling in love with what you're doing, and serving others."

Putting Together a Presentation

Over one hundred direct sales companies represent products from dust mops to faux-pearl jewelry, diet-food supplements to custom-made clothing, bubble bath to vacuum cleaners. But all of these products have one thing in common—all need to be sold.

What, then, is the best way to sell them?

Most companies will train you to sell their products to best effect. This training is based on the experience of successful salespeople who have discovered techniques that best handle the particular objections that are unique to each product. Usually each company will recommend a personal style and approach, and teach you what has worked best for their products. Whether your company operates on a party plan through ''classes,'' or on a one-to-one basis, you'll need to master the company's script, as well as the basics of successful selling.

The components of every good presentation are detailed below. They are:

Getting Attention

Since you've put a lot of effort into learning your selling lines (prepared by the company or improvised by you) and more effort into making the call to get the appointment in the first place, make every second count now that you're face to face with your prospect. I can guarantee that your customer hasn't been anxiously waiting for this opportunity, even though you may think it's a great one. In fact, she may not be in the mood to hear about your wonderful spot removers or cream blushers at all.

In a group of six or more at a party plan or class, some women might be distracted, irritated, or generally turned off for one reason or another, and not be really interested in the purpose of the evening's meeting. Whoever she is, wherever she is—at her own home or that of the party-plan hostess—you'll need to *get her attention and hold it*. You can do this in two simple ways. The first is small talk.

Learning the art of small talk will earn you great rewards. Small talk is opening, easygoing chatter that reduces any tension and allows a chance for interaction before you make a sales presentation. Essentially, you're establishing *rapport*. Tell an amusing anecdote, ask a question about the person's hobby, give a compliment (to her, about her husband/children/dog/home), introduce a nonargumentative comment about a sports event, or whatever seems appropriate. Small talk, no matter the topic, *begins* selling dynamics.

In her excellent book, *Winning by Negotiation*, Tessa Albert Warschaw wrote, ". . . for most of us, small talk is the social lubricant to get us working smoothly with one another. It's not simply a form of mutual courtesy by which we help one another relax. It's a means to gain important knowledge." One key to mastering small talk is to phrase questions or comments in a form that requires a more descriptive answer, not just a yes or no. An example: "Joan, I understand you've taken up tennis. What got you interested in it?" Joan will most likely reveal information about herself in response and feel more connected to you personally.

Keep small talk small—no personal crises and devote only a few minutes to it so the subject doesn't become distracting.

Get Them Interested In Your Product

You'll want to make a smooth transition from small talk to talking business—the *purpose* of your appointment. When you're selling a product that could tie in with the subject of your introductory chat, it's a natural transition. For example: You learned Joan plays tennis. If you're selling cosmetics or skin care products, suggest a sunblocker or soothing foot cream; if your product is health foods or diet programs, mention how it can supply the nutrients she needs while providing energy; if detergents are your line, suggest a whitener. Two ways you might approach it: "You're spending much more time in the sun now, Joan, and that's got to be a little hard on your skin. I know you'll be interested in a great sunblocker like ours. It's *very* popular. Women tell me that their husbands use it, too, when they're outdoors for long periods. You'll love it when you try it." *OR*, "You mentioned that you start losing energy midway into your game. I know just what you mean. I used to fade out during my exercise classes and found it was because of how I was eating beforehand. ABC Health Food Supplements, though, changed my energy level enough to make a big difference. I'd love for you to try the basic supplement for two weeks. I'll call you in a week to check how you're doing with it. You'll like how good this product makes you feel."

You'll hold a customer's interest when you *introduce a benefit and stress it*. Joan wants to know what will help her look and feel better. Tell her how, then show her how by demonstrating the product, if that's a practical part of your presentation. Many companies have visuals to accompany presentations, such as Shaklee salespeople who show film strips. Visual aids tend to help customers connect more immediately with what the products or the career can do for them.

Wrap up this segment of your presentation by giving Joan a briskly paced summation of your product. Don't speed-speak, but list the relevant benefits, details, and prices in an enthusiastic tone. This reminds her why she should buy from you! Finally, *guarantee* your product if you can. Stress the product's *advantages*, positive *values*, *popularity*, why it's a *time-saver* (if that's the case), how it's *economical* (if that's a true feature), why she'll be pleased with this *discovery* (she didn't know your company made this product until now), how it's been *scientifically tested* or that it's the company's most *up-to-date* product.

Ask For The Order

Joan must believe in you and your product, yet she wants to sell herself on it, not be sold by you. At this point in the example you want to steer Joan toward taking action and giving you the order. There's only one way to do that: A*sk for it!* "Is there any reason why we can't start you on the ABC supplements today?" However, Joan may not be ready to buy, and in this case you must be prepared with such a "trial closing" statement. This allows Joan to voice any objections not yet satisfactorily answered. Trial closings are an exchange of opinions and diplomatic rebuttals that do not make the customer "wrong" or argue her point. If you do, you'll then have her decision: NO. The skilled salesperson views doubts and objections as a way to strengthen one's selling position to get the order. How do you do this?

Anticipate objections. By doing so, you'll learn how to turn them around to your advantage. By thinking them *through* beforehand, you can have an answer ready. Let's take a closer look.

Listen to Customer Response

What's holding Joan back from making an immediate decision? Unless you probe with leading questions and personalize the sales presentation to focus on *her* needs and insure *her* interest, she'll get up and bid you good day. Always remain in good humor. "You mustn't let the objection strike you as a rejection of you *or* the company," advises Marlys Skillings, a National Sales Director with Mary Kay based in Larkspur, Colorado. "Instead, look at the objection as if it were a question, then answer it with a solution or an idea. When you learn how to overcome objections, I think you'll hit upon one of the *key* reasons for success in direct sales."

Marlys believes that people can get stuck in objections and make them ponderous, impenetrable problems—like trying to walk a mile through wet cement. It's her positive attitude toward the word *no* or even *maybe* that's made her one of the top people in our company.

Marlys—who shares a similar work history to mine (first modeling, then working as a talk-show hostess in Sioux City, Iowa), came from a broken home where, because of circumstances, she was obliged to move from friend's house to friend's house for a few months at a time. "When I was fourteen years old and until I was seventeen, I had to be resourceful just to live," she said. "I learned a lot about how to fit in, what I had to do to adjust and, most of all, how *not* to feel rejected. I think I may have been fortunate in dealing with rejection at an early age and developing a positive attitude about moving on." Marlys married at eighteen and was a grandmother at thirty-eight. Family has always been important to her, but so is her career. Marlys has set her sights to earning $20,000 a *month*, within the next three years, up from her 1986 total of $11,000 a month—and she believes no objections can dissuade her. She's committed to positive rein-forcement of her strong points, and a constant growth pro-cess to keep handling objections constructively.

I strongly agree on this point. Success depends on not taking objections personally! Objection tends to weaken some of us and we back off. The pity is, the second we agree with a customer's objection, we've generally lost the sale. The problem is in recognizing that "rejection" is sometimes only the customers' way of asking if *they're* making a right decision. They just need reassurance. They want to feel they under-stand everything about the product and how it will benefit them. It's just that the "questions" are often phrased in a neg-ative manner and so we may flinch. If we don't learn to over-come objections without taking them personally, we begin to back off and get intimidated. Some people who aren't ready to buy will just keep digging up one objection after the other to discourage us. But you can win the sale! Take the opportu-nity to *resell* your customers by listening to their objections. Remember, rejection may be nothing but a request for more information.

Let's return to Joan now, who is posing an objection she thinks is a real one. You're selling ABC Health Food Supple-ments. She says: "I don't see how ABC Supplements are any better than the XYZ Protein Tabs I pick up at the store."

Since you're selling food supplements, you'll have this marketing information for Joan. The issue of comparisons will always be raised no matter what you sell—vitamins, cosmet-ics, vacuum cleaners, jewelry, or package tours to Brazil. Joan was informed earlier in your sales pitch about how ABC Sup-plements are a superior product. She wants to hear it again, or she may not have quite understood the subtle difference between ABC's formula and the commercial variety she finds at the supermarket.

You have already told Joan, but tell her again: "It's an interesting story, as you know, Joan. ABC's were formulated by a team of Swiss doctors who wanted to pack the most nutrition in the most convenient form—the tablet. ABC's are concentrated foods, like ones the astronauts take on their trips to outer space, not just clever chemistry. The great thing about ABC's, Joan, is that you'll feel the difference in your energy level immediately. You'll love ABC's . . . and I also have a feeling that you're a woman who'd want the best product for her money, wouldn't you?"

This response answers Joan's question and restates a benefit. Asking her a question she will most likely agree with, placed at the *end* of your statement, draws her back in. Of course, Joan *could* raise another objection following agreement with you: "Sure, I want the best for my money, but . . ."

This is okay. As long as Joan brings up objections that you feel aren't time wasters, but are sincere efforts to be sold, *hear her out.* Joan may return to the issue of price, or real need for the product, wanting to know who else has taken ABC's and how they felt about them. Answer each objection so that it brings Joan closer to saying YES. Stay in control of the meeting and in control of your emotions. Persist! I read of one great salesman who declared to a prospect: "I'll stay here all night to answer your questions and I won't leave until I have the order." You may not be so openly confident in word, but be so in deed.

It is true that objections sometimes do try your patience and test your skill at salesmanship. Instead, soften your disagreement by posing your statement positively, then provide the information. "I know just why you'd believe that and why you'd bring that point up again. ABC's have . . ." (Don't say, "Really, Joan. I already told you why three times. It still comes out the same answer.") Some objections can introduce another slant on the product that doesn't relate to it at all. Handle these by saying, "That's an interesting approach, Joan, and you'll find that ABC's are the perfect food supplement to take all year long. . . ." (Don't say, "I never heard of weather having an effect on ABC's.")

All roads, cleared of objections, lead to "closing" the sale. This will be the moment of truth. You're going to ask Joan for the sale by being direct, positive, and clear in your intention. This is where many people trip over their own feet. Few sales close themselves. You'll have to take some risks and *get the order*!

Closing Strategies

You may have won a friend in Joan, charmed her, helped her spend a pleasant half hour or so in an otherwise dreary day, but if she still says, "I'll think about it. Call me in a few weeks," you haven't fulfilled your purpose—getting Joan to sign on the dotted line. You haven't closed the sale yet, but you will.

Closing strategies are subtle and require attention and practice. Through experience you'll sense when to coax the customer into action and when to pull back a bit and not close prematurely. There is a lot of psychology involved. You want to be positive, expressive, and *direct*. Think in terms of winning the sale, then do something that gets it.

Experts have examined the process of closing in minute detail, from practitioners of the mystical approach (knowing what someone wants before *they* even acknowledge it and how to sell them) to the more insistent, hard-boiled hard sell

("You're not leaving until you buy this!") and all manner of grace, intuition, and skillful salesmanship between the two extremes. Experience has taught me that closing a sale successfully relies on these final points most of all:

Positive reinforcement: Making a sale is great, but making a sale once doesn't insure ongoing business. Therefore, unless the customer feels good about the product and how will benefit her, she's not going to buy and *continue* buying. And the *continued* sale is the most important one. Remind her of how your products benefit her and how they will make her life better: she'll look radiant after a facial and with new make-up, the jewelry is flattering and makes unique gifts, the products she needs are conveniently shipped to her door, her children deserve the finest educational reference books.

Let's close a sale with Mary Kay Cosmetics. I'd tell my customer, Veronica: "You look wonderful, don't you think?" Veronica will agree. "This is what you've tried today. Everything is formulated for your skin type and is perfect for you. So let's look over these items and decide what you'll need." I will take out an order form and begin to fill it out. Then I like to add, "Veronica, you deserve it all. I know you agree."

Assume, use emotion, or ask: Closing a sale works on a number of levels of assertiveness. Which one you opt for depends on the tenor of your sales meeting and with whom you are dealing.

◆ **Assumption** implies that you reveal no doubts to the customer that she'll buy. Your attitude is positive. Let's assume a close with Veronica again: "These are the products you've tried today, Veronica, and they're perfect for you. Is there any reason why we can't start you with the complete set? You'll love it." I would remind her again that she's making a correct decision and that she deserves the pleasure and compliments she'll get from using these cosmetics.

♦ Direct sellers know that people will often buy more on **emotion** than logic, so you'll need to introduce subtle emotional arguments that will help persuade the sale to happen. Sum up for her why your products are superior. To make the sale: *Be her friend to the end. Make it simple for her to buy.*

I'll illustrate by closing a sale, using Mary Kay products. Suppose my customer brings up an objection at zero hour— an objection she hadn't mentioned earlier—price, spending the money at all, she doesn't really need makeup, whatever. Use the objection to close the sale. Let's take expenditure: "I know how you feel, Veronica. We women tend to think, well, we've got a few extra dollars and baby needs shoes, or as you said, your kitchen could use new curtains. Veronica, you work so hard, you deserve a little pampering. You deserve to feel and look good, too. You'll get those curtains, you know you will, but do something nice for you. Tell me how much you'd feel comfortable spending today and we can go with that for now."

Relieve her of feeling pressured by suggesting a few products to start. Let her make a minor decision and feel right. Whatever the compromise, you can be sure that when you next contact Veronica, you'll get a larger order.

♦ Finally, **asking.** Superstars of closing are known for their candid ability to openly, assertively, and neatly ask for the sale. If you're of this hardier persuasion, go to it and ask for the sale: "I'm putting you down for the set, Veronica. I know you're going to love our skin care products." Order forms create a sense of finality. Produce the form as you ask for the sale, never taking your eyes off the customer. Hand her the pen and show her where to sign. Ask for the money: "You choose how you'd like to pay—check, cash, or credit card."

Points to remember about closing:

♦ Summarize the benefits of the product.

♦ Listen to the customer.

♦ Continue with the feeling of confidence, trust, and friendship that you established during the meeting. Don't become cooler, colder, or more "business-like" because you're nearing the end of the sale.

♦ Let the customer buy from you.

♦ Ask for the sale in whatever way most suits you, but ask!

Follow-up

Any effort put into a sale hasn't much value without follow-up. What a pity it would be to lose what you've worked so hard to gain. Follow-up implies ongoing communication with a customer or recruit; it indicates courtesy, interest in a customer's needs; it allows for problem solving and even establishes friendship. Follow-up keeps you attentive and on your toes to how you're running your business. Thorough follow-up helps you sustain the relationship. The payoff is just good business, and the reward is a successful career in direct sales.

Follow-up applies to these situations:

◆ **Thank-you notes or calls:** Graciousness is never inappropriate or old-fashioned. Thank your customer for the order.

◆ **Confirming appointments:** Many salespeople worry about cancelations, but since they are typical to the business, be prepared. The initial booking process varies from company to company as does the manner of confirming an appointment at the time it is made. You might be told to follow up with a reminder card, but almost under *no* circumstance would I suggest you call. This can give them an easy enough chance to cancel.

◆ **Orders, reorders:** Your business depends on new and ongoing trade. A customer might have passed something by because of a limited budget. Call and ask if she'd like to place the order for that item now. Remind her how much she liked it and how it suited her, or how she can win it free if that's part of your company policy.

Sometimes, living in a smaller community allows for a more informal approach to selling. You can ask people to pick up orders at your house (rather than having you deliver them), and, while they're there, suggest they take a look at the rest of your line again. If you've got *new* products to show, or if the company is having a sale on certain items, take the opportunity of a customer's visit to increase business beyond her just reordering. Never forget the "power of suggestion."

◆ **Recruiting:** Perhaps you met someone the previous night, a week ago, a month ago, someone you thought right for a direct sales career. She/he may have turned you down, said "maybe," or suggested you try again. Follow-up calls remind them that you're thinking of them as potential business partners. Use this call to make an appointment to discuss a sales career.

Four of my strongest people were all eventually recruited by me because I persisted with follow-up calls. Each woman said the career didn't seem *quite* right—but she didn't actually say no. I had a good feeling that Mona Holte, Marlys Skillings, Fern Hendricks, and Maureen Yantzer were each perfect for this business and I told them so. Not one of these women was living in Minneapolis, so I sent notes or called, especially if I was driving through or near their home cities. Finally, one by one, each said in her own way, "I'm ready!"

Without these follow-up calls, I would have lost them to either another recruiter or another profession. Now these women are my top producers and without them, I would have a much, much smaller business.

◆ **Ask for referrals:** Very few customers volunteer names when they buy from you. It's up to you to scout people. Ask for referrals from satisfied customers. Most direct sales companies provide incentives for referrals—small cash awards or percentages of the sale made, or gifts. In fact, the four above-mentioned women who are my top producers were *all* referrals.

Points to Remember About Sales

◆ Once in a while, history is made by someone who does everything right the first time out and never has a moment of self-doubt ever after. The rest of us need experience, practice, an upbeat attitude, and persistence. **Give yourself time to achieve your goals.**

◆ We all make mistakes. We all have disappointing days. But subsequent good days will make up for those lapses. Give yourself permission to flop now and then—**you don't have to be perfect!** Connect to those errors and don't deny them, then set them straight as gracefully as you can.

◆ Take your business seriously, but **keep a sense of humor about yourself.**

◆ We may be tempted to want to have the person who has recruited us—or a manager of a company—along with us and actually have him/her transact the sale instead of doing it ourselves. I've always felt that confidence is weakened when you delay honing your skills by letting others do for you what you should be doing for yourself. If you're deeply worried about what to do and say the first few times out, perhaps your recruiter or manager can invite you to watch him or her in action. Don't shortchange yourself from getting the experience you need. **Do it yourself.**

◆ **Keep a goal in sight.** Nothing is more motivating than inching (or bounding) toward the kind of success you design yourself.

◆ The measure of your rewards will be **the quality of your involvement.** I can't tell you how much money you're going to earn in sales, but if you describe your plan of action to me and tell me how many hours a week you're willing to invest, I'll know exactly where you'll be in two years . . . three years . . . ten years. And so will you! Think about it!

◆ **Attend weekly sales meetings.** This is imperative for all direct sales people—especially those who don't have a clearly structured day. Meetings keep you on target, let you share ideas and clarify solutions to common problems. It's your support group. When you're down, you need the meeting. When you're *up*, the meeting needs you!

Recruiting and Training

"**I** thought recruiting was the worst part of the business and it scared me the most," said Elizabeth Hagen, a Mary Kay Sales Director based in Marina Del Rey in California. "Recruiting meant I had to convince people to do what I was doing. But since I was so unsure of what I was doing, I actually felt they'd be *lowering* themselves if they let me recruit them!"

Elizabeth's attitude about recruiting changed so dramatically that she eventually went on to place fifth in the country in sales for Mary Kay a few years ago. But initially she had to understand the business. "With a little experience and success selling the products, pretty soon I felt more comfortable about the whole business. I found I *could* meet my financial goals easily," she added. "I was going along steadily. Then someone in the company suggested that I take the next step and start recruiting because that was where I could really make money. It became obvious to me that this person was right—I was sitting on a *fabulous* business opportunity. All I had to do was look up! That concept became the best selling point in recruiting others—business *opportunity*."

Elizabeth is my daughter—the one who generously rounded up seven of her school chums and participated in my very first direct sales experience. She was also the one who believed her destiny lay somewhere other than in selling "stuff in pink boxes." Before joining Mary Kay, Elizabeth had gone through a number of occupations over her first three years after college—from ski hostess to a traditional nine-to-five job in advertising.

"I was making bologna sandwiches at a lodge in Aspen, Colorado, when I left college," Elizabeth said. "It wasn't a whole lot classier than what I thought Mary Kay represented, but I felt better *not* being a salesperson." She "weakened" at one point and let me recruit her, but, as she tells it, "I didn't like it at all! I lasted about two weeks and thought that was enough. Then things changed over a few years. I got married, had a child, and we needed money." This time, Elizabeth *asked* me to recruit her. "I think we go through stages where our needs change," she explained. "I was ready then to try Mary Kay. It took nearly a year for me to get there and recruit, but I did it. Recruiting soon became what excited me about the business. It wasn't long before I wound up with terrific people who created a lot of terrific business activity of their own!"

When she started selling, Elizabeth set a goal of "spending money for the week." That year, it amounted to $150 a week or about $600 a month, which supplemented a before-taxes salary of $13,000 a year selling advertising space for an Aspen magazine. Since her husband at the time was starting his own business, every dollar helped. In her second year, she earned $33,000 with Mary Kay alone—commission dollars earned from percentages on sales from her own business and those of her recruits. In her fourth year, she more than doubled that!

Not everyone who works with a company offering multi-level or override commissions, bonuses, or rewards for recruiting feels moved to do so. Many people in Shaklee and Amway (to name just two) are content just to sell (and buy) and get a commission (or discounts) on their inventories. But what they've passed up! It may take a bit more motivation or sense of adventure or ambition to get inspired and take the next step as Elizabeth did and *recruit*, but it's worth the effort. It's almost a waste of opportunity not to at least give it a whirl when the company's policy encourages it and the money is there for the making.

One top Amway distributor told me that her recruiter actually *neglected* to tell her she could build a business by recruiting! Seems impossible to believe, but it happened to Sylvia Wolfe, who's now a "Diamond Direct" distributor, a position that establishes her as one of the more successful in the company. Sylvia lives in Palmer, Alaska, and despite "one main road running north and south and early problems with communication and shipping twenty-one years ago," she managed to bring the Amway opportunity to Alaska, after being the first in that state to sign up.

"When I started out, the company was about four years old," Sylvia said. "I was doing okay making extra money selling retail and so busy taking care of my three children that I didn't bother to check and see what Amway offered. I only knew about selling and thought that was all there was. The man who recruited me had come up from Michigan, and whatever was on his mind when he got to Alaska, it didn't include telling me about sponsoring others!"

The pastor of her church traveled to Michigan about a

year later and decided to drop in on Amway headquarters in Ada. "He got so excited by the plant and the possibilities, he came back and showed me the marketing plan and how to sponsor. That was in 1965," she added.

Sylvia approached recruiting with a good attitude. "I decided I deserved success, so I sat down and studied the marketing plan until I knew it thoroughly. Then I made calls and explained it to *anyone* who'd listen. I was persistent." Sylvia estimates that she recruited about fourteen people a year. "That's not a particularly high number," she said, "but they're great and work so well." One reason for Sylvia's success with Amway's multilevel format is that she developed a training program for the people she recruited: "I wound up being very good at motivation. I learned I could fire people up to believe in the dream and help them make it happen."

It *is* a dream for many of us but one we've got the *power* to make come true.

Why Recruit?

Recruiting is both a subtle art and a simple system. It involves using your judgment to decide who would be right for your business, and also means creating a wide network of people, who, you hope, are equally interested in success. Additionally, you'll want to recruit for some or all of these reasons:

- ◆ To bring others with whom you'd like to work into the business. You're doing them a favor!

- ◆ To offer others a wonderful business opportunity

- ◆ To perfect your sales ability—persuading others not only to buy a product, but sell it too

- ◆ To increase your yearly income to meet your dream or exceed it

- ◆ To commit to the career of direct selling by taking advantage of every opportunity the company offers

- ◆ To make the effort and gain recognition from the company as well as a great sense of accomplishment when you've met their goals and yours.

When you recruit, others make money and you increase your earnings too. You're sharing your success . . . *doing them a favor.* I really believe this. Elizabeth was typical—she thought she was imposing on people. Not so! Through enthusiasm, technique, and information anyone can build a huge network of recruits who will eventually (just like Elizabeth) reap the rewards of that favor.

Companies encouraging recruitment all have their own special formats, ideas, and general conversational suggestions for those of us who love the challenge of recruiting. However, I know the companies all share some of these basic precepts.

Who to Recruit and Where to Find Them

Years ago, I recruited a minister's wife from Bismarck, North Dakota, and helped start her career with Mary Kay, but Mona never got very far. When she and her husband moved to Des Moines, she dropped out and started raising a family. Something about Mona Holte held my interest in her lapsed career, though. In my travels through the Midwest, I'd always send her a card. In it I'd say I was thinking about her, reminding her that I thought she'd be great back in sales, tell her when I'd be in town, and suggest that perhaps we could meet and chat about the business.

Very politely, Mona always declined. I persisted in the mildest way, affirming again that I had faith in her and that when she was ready, I'd be there to help her along. One day, she was ready to start working again and called me to report that she'd recruited four people. I cheered her on and said, find three more and you can go into "qualification"—a Mary Kay term for the first level of management. Mona made it! She couldn't believe she'd gone from nothing to something wonderful in about five weeks, after a great gap of inactivity.

What was fascinating to me about Mona was that she wasn't quite sure if this career was for her—but I knew she was right and played a hunch. I waited for her and *persisted* for years, and she came through for herself and for me. Now she's one of the top people in the company.

I met Mona at a Mary Kay skin care class, one of the more perfect places to find recruits. She was an attendee, though usually the most likely candidate to become a recruit is the host or hostess. This is the person who offers his or her home for the evening and is willing to invite friends to come over. These people are already participating in the business even in this limited way. In fact, they're receiving a gift or small percentage of the evening's sales for their help. Many times these people are shy about speaking up, and often, they're waiting to be formally asked into the business. A rule here is to always ask your host or hostess if he or she wants to join the business.

Friends and relatives are the first to come to mind (after considering customers) when you decide to recruit. Well-meaning friends and family may be the more recalcitrant "dis-approvers" who totally resist all your efforts to interest them in your career. Move on briskly and don't let their negativity get to you. Then again, your family may be the smiling, kind-hearted "approvers" who sign up just to please you, but thereafter forget what business they're in. Don't feel too dis-appointed in their performance and move on just as briskly. With family, you need to be brutally frank with yourself about *who* and *what* they are (hard workers, procrastinators, enthusi-astic, blamers, supersensitive to rejection, whatever) and what you can expect their true involvement to be.

Try your friends on the idea of selling the benefits of re-cruiting. Some might be bored with their jobs or perhaps they've suddenly become aware that they are in dead-end po-sitions at their companies and that they're going nowhere fast. Others may just want to earn extra money. Let them know about the opportunities available in direct selling.

Opportunities for recruitment can present themselves in surprising places! In fact, direct selling gained a new recruit in Mary Ann Schoudel, when she read a version of this book when it was being clean-typed by a friend. Mary Ann, a single parent who had just turned forty, had been trying over the years to pursue an acting career, supporting herself and her son with secretarial jobs, working at "trade shows," and taking on free-lance typing assignments at home for extra money. Professionally, she felt she was at a standstill. "When I read through this book, it dawned on me that direct sales offered me a chance I couldn't get anywhere else," she said. "The more I thought about it, the more I liked the idea of a business that was *mine*. I was always a conscientious worker, and I thought, why not put that energy to work for me. Deep down, it struck me—either I could go with it or continue on the way I was. So I decided, what did I have to lose?"

At the time, Mary Ann's sister was seriously ill, and she was very conscious of health, health products, and nutritional regimens. In deciding to choose a company, Mary Ann went with Shaklee—one direct sales leader which markets vitamins and nutritional supplements, among other products. Mary Ann had met a Shaklee distributor socially, and only had to call her to be recruited. Now a supervisor with the company, Mary Ann says, "One bonus to direct sales for me was that it's also given me direction. I'd never set goals before, sure I'd never reach them. This business helps me set goals, and with the support system of other Shaklee people behind me, I'm motivated to do well. Finding this career came as a surprise to me, and it's changed my life—*un*surprisingly!"

As you can see, you must be alert to possibilities when you least expect them. You can find recruits in locations you probably wouldn't think could hold such treasure. I've known representatives who've made initial contact with eventual recruits in airport lounges while waiting for a runway to be cleared of snow, at a wedding, while sitting in the bleachers at a Little League game, at acting auditions, and on a long line at the bank on a Friday afternoon.

Over the years, I've developed an eye for what I call "sparklers"—women who are animated and have a positive aura about them, just plain "good vibes." I've dined in restaurants and spotted such a woman across a room and, deciding right there on a hunch, I've been guilty of actually following her into the ladies room! There I casually strike up a conversation, give her a compliment about her skin, tell her I'm in the skin care business, offer to give her a complimentary facial, and try to get her number for an appointment and eventually recruit her. If she says no, at least I know I tried—our paths may cross again. But a yes can change my life and hers. As with other chance opportunities like these, they must be followed up quickly by a meeting with the potential recruit so you can demonstrate products and describe in detail the company's marketing strategy.

Don't overlook the husband of your beautician, the wife of the garage mechanic, the mother of your baby-sitter, the sister of your accountant, your postman, a business partner, even your boss. Don't forget that your best customer could be your next surefire recruit. That's how I joined Mary Kay. My recruiter decided to try and recruit her best customer and got me!

No one is improbable as long as you "commit to a plan of action," said Jafra Cosmetics super saleswoman Ilene Lawler. Ilene was not only Jafra's first district director—the top spot— but the company's founders thereafter used *her* 1968 sales record as the criterion for earning the title! How did she do it?

"I always thought my strength was in selling the products, which I love," Ilene told me from her home in Agoura, California. "I also believed that sponsoring others was *not* one of my strong points. I'd been with Jafra since late 1959 and until 1980, I didn't have the answer to why that was. Then I figured it out—I kept telling myself that I wasn't any good at sponsoring! And I believed it. I made a decision to change."

Ilene began with a plan. She wrote out an "affirmation" or commitment to call one person every day and offer the Jafra opportunity. She had no exact number of recruits in mind when she started out, but her goal was to speak to someone, *anyone*, every day and "never let the commitment slip, no matter what. I started by asking my regular customers the simplest question—one I hadn't asked them before: 'Have you ever considered doing this, too?' Some said no, but some said yes," Ilene told me.

From there, she talked to people wherever she could. Some were more accessible—the person looking for a new career or part-time job, or friends, relatives, and neighbors—and others were professionals who were already at some level of achievement.

Before her written "affirmation," Ilene had brought in an average of seventeen people a year. Once her plan was drawn up and carried out "without allowing myself any excuses to miss a day," she counted fifty new recruits at the end of the year! Since then, she's sponsored thirty to forty new people a year.

Anyone who wants to recruit can! "You must have a plan or a strategy," Ilene advised. "It doesn't have to be complicated, but you have to really *want* to do it. Then you must have a *reason*—your motivation. I wanted to do it and my reason was that I believed that others deserved a chance with Jafra."

After twenty-seven years with the company, Ilene reflected: "I was not extremely successful when I started. In over seventy-five classes my first year, not one brought in over $40 in sales. Then one day in 1960, everything turned around for me. What I was doing moved from my head to my heart. I had been harboring a thread of doubt about the products, and that was keeping me back. Once I believed in the product wholeheartedly, I knew I could meet any goal. The secret of my success," she said, "is that I never quit."

One tangible *result* of her success is that Ilene's recruits and their recruits have made her division number one in Jafra six times.

The lesson is a simple one: any place where people congregate should yield at least one person who'll ask questions about your career if you bring it up. When that happens, it's a good sign. Indifference is never encouraging but interest is! Keep talking about your career wholeheartedly and its unlimited growth potential.

That's your drawing card.

How to Recruit

When you recruit people to join your company, keep your objective in mind: You want to *sell a career to people who have already bought and love your product*. Therefore, if you can sell, you can recruit.

Recruiting asks your prospects to make a decision that will change the way they live, how they schedule their days, how they set goals, how they interact with people, how they determine how much money they can make.

This is not a minor request! You'll need to be an expert on the business, a friend, a psychologist, an older brother/sister, and a mind reader to your about-to-be recruit. You'll need to be completely aware of establishing a *positive attitude, a professional approach*, and an *atmosphere of trust*. It will all fall into place for you when you try it yourself.

The following situations and suggested comments present a generally accurate overview of the recruiting session. Some stages of recruiting will take longer than others—and this will depend upon the number of people, the disposition and inclination of the people you'd like to recruit, how much time you'll have, and so forth. To make the process as clear as possible, I'll use the character of "Jane," a married midwestern woman of forty, and try to recruit her. To simplify matters, I'll use the Mary Kay company as her career opportunity, but you can adapt the information to suit other company formats.

So, to begin. If you were recruited, remember how you felt at the time someone asked you to join the company. You probably

◆ Asked questions

◆ Voiced objections

♦ Expressed doubt

♦ Required approval

♦ Expected your recruiter to listen to you.

Understand how Jane feels now and open with a compliment ("Jane, I've been thinking about this meeting and have really been looking forward to it"). Then compliment her again ("I couldn't help thinking about how perfect you'd be for this career"). Chat for a short while about things in general, then follow with *another* compliment ("You have a wonderful sense of humor/a really interesting outlook/a sensitive point of view, so . . ."). This last compliment leads up to the fourth one—asking her to talk about herself in confidence-building terms (". . . so, tell me more about you. What do you like best about yourself? I can tell that you're great with people!")

Give Jane permission to openly express her finer points. Assure Jane that it's not a matter of bragging, but simply acknowledging positive qualities that can help her create a better life. Being able to handle people diplomatically and kindly is as valuable a skill as typing 130 words a minute. Get her to say what's right with her own world and *listen*. Jane will recruit herself by listening to her own voice reinforcing a belief in herself and her assets. That's why we want *her* to listen.

I believe, in fact, that the real process of successful recruiting begins with *listening* to others. When you listen *attentively* to someone and respond with a smile, a nod, an empathetic few words, and a number of sincere compliments at the beginning of your meeting together, you are halfway to recruiting her or him. Why? Everyone has someone to talk to, but it doesn't mean that that someone is *listening*. Listening with genuine interest establishes *trust* and puts others at their ease. They know why you're there, after all, and are perhaps a little intimidated. Be generous with your attention.

Let's return to Jane. Suppose she's recounted her assets and feels at ease with you. You need to probe a bit more now and take note of her needs. Does she need money, recognition, something to fill her time, something to care about? Does she seem competitive—does she need to win or can she lose? Ask yourself: "What would she want from direct sales?"

You want to get her talking by directing the conversation toward questions that require information-giving answers, not yes or no only answers. The more Jane talks and you listen, the more you'll learn about why she'd be right for this career. Often, people respond with surprisingly candid bits of information that will soon help you deal with the toughest part of recruiting—overcoming objections. You need to be really attentive here. Do her objections ring true or do they sound to you like excuses?

So let's assume Jane is relaxed and talking. She may disclose her economic problems or financial goals. She might reveal her outlook on life—whether she's fatalistic, moderate politically, religious, a risk taker, or conservative about accepting new ideas, or maybe a little of all of these. If Jane is married, she will most likely tell you her husband's feelings about working women. Jane may provide you with information about how much power her husband has in deciding her future. But . . . what you want to hear before you pull out recruiting notebooks or flip charts or filmed visual aids is her opinion of direct sales:

◆ If it's favorable or neutral, you'll have a better chance to recruit her. Be enthusiastic about her interest.

♦ If it's tinged with doubt or negative, be happy you found out immediately. As long as she's *willing to hear your presentation* about the business, and doesn't show you the door, proceed with your recruiting strategy. Draw her in by reminding her of her good qualities and what she'd bring to the business.

Okay. We've listened to Jane and discovered that she's tantalized by the idea of the career, but unable to imagine herself actually doing it. Jane needs to get some basic information from you immediately. You need to tell her *what the company has to offer her and what she brings to the job*. Then, by using visual aids (notebooks, films, or whatever the company provides) you'll describe and clarify the company's marketing plan so Jane understands how she can build a career or solid financial future, and, at the same time, gain the personal extras that go with success—self-esteem, recognition, and leadership.

As you turn the pages of the recruiting notebook, probably Jane will be trying to digest growth charts and marketing strategies, the company's policy for earning commissions, bonuses, or rewards, the actual scope of the products, and in the case of the Mary Kay recruiting notebook, pictures of what gifts are in store for her at each level of achievement. (Many other companies share this procedure. They're aware of the psychological impact a photo of the *actual* item can have on someone—not just the word.) There are furs, a pink Buick or Cadillac. There are pearls or diamonds, and there's even a photograph of Mary Kay Ash usually taken with the person who's doing the recruiting. (When my recruiter showed me a picture of Mary Kay, I was stunned to discover she existed—not like a big red spoon representing Betty Crocker!)

Here's where your recruiting skills really begin to be exercised. Earlier, when Jane spoke about her life, she happened to mention that she and her husband just took out a second mortgage. Clearly, Jane needs some financial relief. Income would offset debts one way, but the tax benefits that come with the career help, too. When you operate a direct sales business from home—keep a small home office for paperwork, inventories, meetings, etc.—you may legitimately claim that room, phone, supplies, and so on as a tax deduction. (More on this later.)

This tidbit of financial information may stir Jane's enthusiasm, but she's still unsure of herself. "*Maaaybe,*" she says doubtfully, referring to the tax breaks. She continues this way:

"But I live in Florida. What would I do with a fur coat? And truly, I'd as soon ride a donkey as drive a pink Cadillac!" I'd happily inform Jane that the company would exchange the coat for a piece of equally valuable jewelry. And in the matter of the trademark pink automobile, we understand if you turn it down and hope you go on to earn enough money to buy a Rolls. The fact is, practically nobody wants a pink Cadillac until it's delivered to the front door. Suddenly it looks almost beige. Still not ready, Jane tells you exactly what she likes and doesn't like about what's been presented to her. If she's not opposed to any company policy and she likes the product and trusts her recruiter, I'd reiterate how I think she'd be great in the business and why she deserves the successes that can come from this career. Then I'd ask her if there was *any reason why we couldn't get started.* I'd want to prepare to close the recruitment meeting and hand her the agreement to sign . . . but Jane may show some discomfort and respond with an objection:

- ◆ I've never sold anything before.

- ◆ I have no time, what with two children at home.

- ◆ I already have two (three) part-time jobs.

- ◆ This is fine for you, not me.

- ◆ I have to ask my husband/My husband won't let me.

Jane believes in her objections, and she's fairly convinced they're what prevent her from signing on. Since these objections sound valid, she's hoping there won't be an argument, and that you, the recruiter, won't feel rejected.

Objections are to be expected in sales and in recruiting. They don't signal failure, but, in fact, are a measure of success. Objections leave the situation open to discussion. You can reassure your recruit-to-be that these objections can be overcome. Objections often hide the real reason your recruit-to-be is stalling. She may be afraid to take a chance. Like most of us, she's comfortable with the familiar and what no longer challenges. She may be afraid of success or failure. Those color photographs of cars, furs, jewels, or the ships that will carry her to exotic ports may intimidate her. What if she only wants to make two or three hundred dollars extra a month for a while and *not* achieve at such a level?

The objections Jane voices are common ones heard by direct sales recruiters in any company. Each objection can be handled successfully.

Overcoming Objections

Begin with the understanding that objections can *help* you reach your goal, whether it's selling or recruiting. As I mentioned before, *response*, especially a response with emotional overtones, is easier to negotiate with than indifference, or an intractable NO! or a convoluted, improbable story or an obvious and insincere excuse. When the objection is *genuine*, you have material to work with.

You'll need to be poised and in control when Jane first voices her objections. She doesn't want to be put on the defensive and you don't want to argue her into signing on. Anyone who's been pressured into a position usually puts all her energy into quitting, not building a business. So you want to take a number of steps to reassure Jane and motivate her to join the company.

♦ Don't interrupt her when she tells you her objection. *Don't* tell her she's foolish to bring a point up or that she's wrong. Listen to what she's got to say. Sometimes, people think out loud and actually talk themselves out of their own objections by the time they finish what they have to say!

♦ Some people hesitate to reveal what they really mean, so it's difficult for you to know exactly what the objection *is*. If you're unsure, restate the objection in simple language *as you understand it*. Invariably, they'll tell you if your understanding is correct.

♦ Try to personally identify with her objections or suggest that you know others who felt as she did. Use the "feel, felt, found" approach. This lets you follow up by describing how you (or another person) overcame that objection and triumphed. Tell her: "I know how you *feel*, I *felt* that way, too, at one time, but you know, Jane, I *found* that —— always works." Solve her problem by example.

♦ If you're unsure of how to handle an objection, tactfully try to delay discussing it. Ask Jane if she has any other questions or feelings about the business—and try to respark some enthusiasm. Sometimes, the extra time will help you better frame your approach to the objection. Other times, your prospect may find the answer to her objection in the discussion you just had and never bring it up again. If she does bring it up, and you're unsure, do the best you can.

Using these principles, let's look at how we'd assuage Jane's five objections:

◆ **I've never sold before:** Jane will probably tell you that she's never even sold Girl Scout cookies. She can't believe that her lack of experience won't hold her back from the opportunities you've enumerated. She thinks she's unqualified for direct sales.

This objection is an emotional one, revealing Jane's doubt about testing herself in a new way. We've all felt as Jane does: "I can't learn to drive . . . cook the way my mother does . . . operate a word processor . . . slam dunk a basketball like my brother Bill." It's not that we've tried, but it's that we've decided a priori, that we *cannot*.

I'm of the mind that Jane *can* and I want her to know why. Since I totally identify with her objection, I'd say, "Jane, I wish I could remember this figure exactly, but I think that about 98 or 99 percent of all Mary Kay beauty consultants never sold a thing before joining the company. Including me. So, I think you'll find that having no sales experience doesn't matter at all. You're starting out like 98 or 99 percent of us, so we understand just how *you* feel and can help you."

Jane will feel better but she's still not convinced: "I don't know if I'm going to be any good at this." And so I'd suggest something like this to her: "Jane, you're going to be just fine, you'll see. And I want you to know I asked you to work with me because I pick winners. Don't forget that you're someone people like and trust. That matters more than anything in selling. So don't worry about experience. You'll learn everything you need to know in the training."

Jane may require one or two more of your efforts to reassure her. Remind her again and again of her good points—the ones she cited and any other you observed over the course of the evening. Emphasize that lack of experience never stopped any champion—who also started at point zero.

◆ **I have no time, what with two children at home:** Thousands of mothers with preschool-age children have built lucrative part-time direct sales businesses yielding full-time incomes, businesses that were run from their homes. Thousands! There's no direct sales company that couldn't claim a good percentage of their successful salespeople who didn't begin with infants on their laps or toddlers underfoot. My own four children were preteen and teenage when I started with Mary Kay. So while they didn't need constant attention and were old enough to participate in their own care, they still needed parental supervision.

Another objection Jane might bring up is an emotional one. She knows how exhausted she is at the end of the day and does not want to add to her work load. She has, though, shown a lot of interest in making extra money and tells us she may give sales a try in five or six years when the children are older. The result of my own unofficial survey reveals an interesting statistic: Of women who entered direct sales when their children *were* older, about 70 percent wish they had begun the career when their children were small! Some women, of course, had not investigated the career earlier, but others who knew of the opportunity and "could have it to live over again," would have signed up a decade or so earlier. Why? One major reward of the career is *positive thinking*—and that always affects home life beneficially.

Jane could be lost to direct sales over a five-year gap unless she's convinced that the time is right . . . right *now*. She doesn't want you to tell her she's not managing her time properly. She's not interested in hearing advice about increasing energy levels or introducing weight-loss programs—unless you are selling vitamins and diet supplements, make her feel good about taking on a new regimen and business at the same time. Solve Jane's problems this way: Identify with her plight. If you have been in her position, what could be better? If not, recall a case to mind and tell her, "I know just what you're going through. . . ." Follow up immediately with a *nonthreatening plan of action*: "Jane, let's get you a sitter for two hours a day for just a few days. I could show you how to make money to pay for the sitter and you'll make a profit, too. You're so right for this business and I think you feel that way, too." If she tells you she'd feel guilty about leaving the children, remind her of a point she mentioned earlier in the evening: "Think about this, Jane. You spend so much time caring for the children. But as you told me earlier, sometimes you miss the stimulation and challenge of the business world. I felt that way, too, when I was just starting out, but found that working a few hours a day changed me so much. You'll see. You'll feel revitalized. And you don't have to dip into the family budget to pay for the sitter, either. Let's start something special for you. . . ."

If Jane wants to ponder this some more, promise to call her back soon. Tell her when and call when you said you would. If you think she's really dynamic and don't want to pass her by, try to arrange a meeting with a few other young mothers who've successfully managed motherhood and entrepreneurship. The best mothers are not necessarily those who are home *all* the time. Mary Kay, herself a mother of three, says of this, "You want motherhood, not smotherhood or otherhood." We don't want to overdo "mothering" or ne-glect children, calling it "encouraging independence." A balance is what counts. For so many of us, the access and stimulation of the business world make us more aware of ourselves and our capabilities—and can help us develop skills we can pass on to our children.

◆ **I already have a job or two (three) part-time jobs:** My recruiter heard me utter the three-part-time-jobs-already objection, but she didn't give up, so sure was she that I'd like Mary Kay products. Marilyn originally offered to demonstrate them and give me a facial, one-to-one, at any time of day, at any place. I suggested eight in the morning at my house to discourage her, but she cheerfully agreed and showed up promptly. And so I found my career, thinking I had no time for it!

In this universe, a number of things are truly unequal among us mortals, but time, above all, is democratic. The Maharajah of Jaipur, Nancy Reagan, your postman, and you each have a twenty-four-hour day. Wealth can't buy an extra hour and impoverishment doesn't shortchange the cycle. One difference between successful and less-than-successful people is that the successful *care* about every minute in the day and how it's lived.

Nothing is more vital to success "than managing *yourself* effectively with respect to time," wrote Harold L. Taylor in his book *Making Time Work for You.* Instead of our worrying that we don't have time "to manage our time," he says, we'll get a lot more accomplished and "move closer to personal and organizational goals" when we manage our lives by knowing what's important and what's not. "We can't wait until we have time to take on another task. We will never have any more time than we have right now. What we have to do is free up some of the time we have by eliminating nonproductive or low-priority activities and quickly replace them with more valuable activities." *Successful people always follow the rule of doing what's important first.*

Busy people are often precisely the ones who are asked to take on another task. If they can't get it done themselves, they'll know to delegate the job to someone who'll fulfill the responsibility. Is Jane one of these people? You think she is.

Jane insists her schedule is too tight. Tell her something like, "Jane, that's why I asked you. You're ambitious, energetic, and you've said on a number of occasions that sales interested you. I don't often prejudge anyone who comes into this business and decide who's going to be great and who isn't. But I feel you're definitely going to be one of our best."

If she keeps to this objection and doesn't bring up another, continue with an invitation to breakfast or lunch, or a meeting after her work day is over. Adjust to her schedule.

If Jane is too overwhelmed by work or family and backs down, end the meeting with a sincere compliment or two that stress your feelings about her worth. Jane is someone most recruiters look for. Keep following up. Send her little notes. Call and remind her of how you liked her and thought she'd be great because the busiest people are often the best. Persist. Chances are, she'll find the time.

♦ **This is fine for you, not me:** Or, **My daughter is looking for a job like yours. What did you say it could pay?** There are cases when it's true—this business suits me perfectly and is entirely inappropriate for another person. In other situations, this rejoinder is more a put-down. Finally, it may be a simple defense. You'll know the difference by the tone of voice.

When I face this (these) statement(s), I'm reminded of two

rules of handling objections: 1) You needn't handle them all so avoid them. 2) Don't argue with, show resentment toward, or insult the prospect. Therefore, I've ignored comments like these and ended the meeting cordially. Other times (using Jane again), I'd feel she might be a bit intimidated and is distancing herself by telling me she's not suited for sales. In that case, I'll take time to inquire a bit more and find out how she really feels. If Jane reveals disinterest, distrust, or dislike for sales and salespeople, I'd invest my recruiting energy on someone less resistant. Personally, I use a little technique that helps me through those occasional harsh "put-downs"—as I turn away, I simply think, "Let her go wrinkle!" referring, of course, to her not using our products.

◆ **I have to ask my husband/My husband won't let me:** This is a delicate situation. Jane may cling to this objection rather than admit she's afraid of taking a risk. She could be telling you how her marriage works, or a combination of both. You need to discover which force dominates, so you can apply some leverage.

Tactfully frame a statement so it questions business knowledge rather than attitude. "I see. Does your husband know a lot about this company? It would be great if he does." Jane will usually inform you that he doesn't know as much as she does. This opening question is nonthreatening and should relax her. Now we can try to discover if the problem stems from Jane or the specter of the "forbidding" husband. You need to use some intuition and size her up as accurately as possible about now, before your next statement. Does Jane seem overly in need of approval or fussing to please others? Does she have a sour edge or appear put upon? If so, she may be too vulnerable for sales. Your answer probably is: Jane's afraid to take a risk and chooses to defer to her husband. But remember, women *do* grow in this area and can have an independent career without threatening a husband.

If she is animated and bright, but timid or hesitant about venturing into business because, she says, of her husband's attitudes, she'll need some reassurance. Jane should know that in other marriages, partners confront similar imbalances of power/control/mutual cooperation. I don't want to make this meeting into a political issue or imply that her husband is a "bad guy" who controls her every decision. I'd try this: "I'd be happy to review the marketing plan with your husband, Jane, so he understands how the company works and what you'd be doing. And, I need to warn you about something that happened to me, too, when I began . . ." (I'd lean in closer to her, as if sharing a confidentiality.) "Well-meaning relatives are *very* good at discouraging us. It happened to me, but I just nodded when everyone said I was crazy to sell and went ahead and made another call. I know you have some of that fight in you."

"I *know* Bob," Jane argues. "He'll *never let me do it.*"

Now, I'd offer arguments in her favor to take home to Bob. "Remember one thing about direct sales, Jane. You pick your hours, and make your own schedule and build your business at your own pace. You're organized and thorough–you said so yourself! Your work life shouldn't in any way interfere with your home life. Direct sales allows us to put our families ahead of our jobs. Bob won't even know you've got a part-time career until he sees the checks you'll be cashing!"

Jane may be unable to articulate *why* her husband won't permit her to start a business. Ask her to find out from him, and ask her again. Remind her that you'd be happy to make a presentation to her husband, at his convenience. "Often,

Jane;' I'd say, "husbands start out saying no to their wives' careers, then eventually wind up in the business, too. I know of a few men who quit a job they didn't like. Their wives made enough money to cushion a mid-life change of occupation without threatening their financial security."

Often by pointing out the benefits to both husband and wife, you win not just a new recruit, but one with a supportive husband.

Closing

This is the moment of truth for both you and Jane. Everything you've said and done up to now has been to fulfill your goal and *close*—that is, recruit her. If Jane is convinced the opportunity is right for her, she will tell you she's ready to sign up. You've succeeded in meeting your goal. Let's say Jane is still a dubious or reluctant recruit-to-be. She has to face a momentous decision about her life. Does she really want to be recruited? She must tell you yes or no. You, however, want to take this meeting to a successful conclusion and skillfully guide Jane along to say yes and "buy" the career. What strategies would work best?

Closing techniques are the subject of entire books and psychological studies—that's how varied, subtle, and unique they are. And as varied as they are, so are their practitioners. Some salespeople are perfectly comfortable in asking for the sale or the career. ("Great, then! It's decided! Right after you sign up, I'll give you all the details about your first training session this coming Saturday.") Others clutch about closing time, no matter how smooth the sales presentation or warm the rapport. They do this by perpetuating discussions of issues that can take them back to point zero. ("Oh, I see. You're still worried about what your husband will say/where to leave the kids/whether you could sell or not . . .)

Studies do reveal that salespeople have a 30 percent higher success rate if they *ask* for the sale, instead of backing down and waiting for the prospect to make the commitment. The same is true for recruiting. You want to *motivate her by making it easy* for her to sign the agreement and feel good about it. You actually have to help her make the decision or make it for her.

These would be my recommendations:

We have something important on our side—Jane hasn't turned you down flat. She's still attentive, listening eagerly, asking questions (or asking them again). You can see that she's excited by the idea of the career. She must make a decision. Yet, she cannot. Her hesitancy most likely reflects self-doubt—a fear that she'll fail/succeed/test her skills in the world and disappoint herself and those around her/create problems with a husband who'll think she's taken a job to compete with him . . . or whatever Jane's worst fear is vis-à-vis this career. I would reassure her again that she'd be great at this. Jane's still listening. Follow the compliment by saying, "So, Jane, is there any reason why we can't get you started now on a part-time basis?"

By suggesting that she sign up on a part-time basis, I've hopefully set her mind at ease. The decision threatens Jane—that's clear enough. But I want her to know that I see no other objections by asking what I hope is a rhetorical question ("Is there any reason why . . .") and that she needn't worry about the career looming before her and consuming her day (". . . on a part-time basis.") Jane will ask what happens when she agrees—how much will it cost her to start out, where will she go for training? Inform her and assure her at the same time.

"Jane, we can get you started immediately when you sign the agreement. Submit your check, then you'll get your showcase and you're ready for training this Saturday. You've made the right decision."

If Jane says, "Where do I sign?" or "Why not?" or "I'm ready!" *stop selling* and hand her the agreement and a pen. My experience has shown that the second my recruit-to-be has the agreement in hand, the best thing is to give her some air! Don't speak about anything but the agreement itself. Move Jane into filling out the form. And when she's involved in the writing of it, it's good to *be quiet*, though I'd chat lightly just to get Jane started with comments like, ". . . the first line asks for your birthdate . . ." Most people feel uncomfortable when others watch them writing, so attend to your own business by quietly packing away papers or samples.

Once Jane has signed and given you the form and her check (if that's the procedure), reassure her again and set an appointment for her first training session.

Perhaps Jane stopped midway into filling out the form to bring up points that troubled her before. They may concern the company's policy about returning the inventory she's bought, or the training; or she may hit a point of extreme personal doubt by listing family crises or upcoming events that would interfere with building a business.

Jane may sincerely want to back out or to stir your support yet again. I'd try to find out what Jane is really thinking by using what is called a *push/pull* technique. This is letting the person go and then seeing if she asks to return. You do this by expressing understanding in a few sentences and agreeing that she's not ready . . . but that's okay! You want to end the meeting on a warm note and let her know that you really *did* think she'd be wonderful for direct sales by adding, for example, "Jane, maybe you're right, this business isn't for you at all.

But I'll keep you in mind and hope we can meet for lunch some time." While talking to her, finish packing your papers or samples at a slow pace—you don't want to distract her from the words. Jane will consider what you've said and most likely take in your accompanying gestures. You've pushed her forward, then you've pulled back. Now it's Jane's move.

If she says, "I just can't right now," believe her and end the meeting.

Conversely, the business may intrigue Jane and she may not want to be left behind. Maybe she doesn't want you to leave just yet. She may restate a question that came up while exploring the marketing plan: "How do I know I'll make money?" My advice is to cheerfully tell her the truth. "If I could promise you'd set the world on fire, I would. But, truly, Jane, we don't know how high you could go unless you give the business a try. Let's take the first step by signing the agreement. Remember, you're in control of your own success and I'll tell you this, I always pick winners and I feel you'd be great at this."

This final speech may be just what Jane needs to hear to sign up.

Push/pull usually elicits a decision one way or the other. People who have great difficulty saying no or trying something new may actually appreciate the technique. You're leaving! Those who require extra attention get it from you and make their decision.

Rosemary Sabatino, Fuller Brush division manager in Orlando, Florida summed up wisely: "Every day, look into the mirror and encourage the person you see there! Be persistently positive. It will not only encourage yourself, but give you what you need to encourage others."

Rosemary's story is an interesting one. She was formally

trained as a medical technician—an occupation she stayed with for seventeen years. After deciding she wanted a career that provided more growth, energy, and positive feedback, she worked with another direct sales company for a year before joining Fuller Brush. She was "surprised" that she liked selling, and even more pleasantly surprised that *recruiting* became what she loved most about direct sales. "What excites me most about recruiting," she told me, "is that I sell people on themselves, not only on the career. I know they can do it! It's great seeing them advance."

Married and the mother of two, Rosemary says that her family comes first with her, and that direct selling did not interfere with her priorities. In fact, it added to her family life because it helped everyone become goal-oriented. She found what mattered most was belief in herself, belief in the products, and setting goals. "A job should be more than something you do from nine to five. Direct sales, I think, gives us the opportunity to get where we want in life—it really can be the great American dream."

Though she had little experience before Fuller Brush, Rosemary took sales training courses. They've helped her understand the dynamics of sales and inspired her to set and reset her goals. "One thing I'm sure about is that you can learn to sell and then teach others. That's what direct sales is all about."

And finally: Sometimes, it helps to take a look, on paper, at why you may or may not want to sign up with a direct sales company. A number of Mary Kay directors, on their own, put together a questionnaire that they give to possible recruits. I think it helps people clarify their motives for wanting to sell while it points up their positive and negative attitudes. I imagine that the questions would apply to any direct sales company, except for one or two that are specifically about beauty care. Here it is:

These are some of the reasons others have chosen to become Mary Kay Beauty Consultants. Which would appeal to you?

1. Gain new friends
2. Improve self-confidence
3. Learn more about improving self-appearance
4. Recognition for being an individual who's capable of running her own business
5. Earn extra income with unlimited capability
6. Earn extra income for family vacations
7. Tax deductions, tax advantages of being self-employed
8. To change my life
9. Because many of the people have God first, family second, career third priorities
10. Flexible hours
11. Helping others look more beautiful and thrill of helping others discover their full potential
12. Positive thinking
13. More time at home with family

What three skills or personality traits do you feel you already have that should be strengths in building your business?

1. _____

2. _____

3. _____

If a skin care class takes 2–3 hours, how many could you hold in one week?

_____

If you were to choose to become a Beauty Consultant, what five people would you select to share with first?

1. _____

2. _____

3. _____

4. _____

5. _____

As far as work goes, I like to:

_____ be the boss

_____ have a boss

When it comes to money:

_____ I handle money well

_____ need help managing money

I prefer to:

_____ be given options but make my own choice of when

_____ make my own daily schedule at work

_____ have a schedule of work to follow

I feel more comfortable when I'm working:

_____ alone

_____ with 2–6 people

_____ with 6–20 people

_____ with 20 or more people

I feel happiest and most self-confident when:

_____

Ways for my friends to make me feel wanted or loved are:

_____

The ways I show others I care are:

_____

Generally speaking, I think I can:

_____ accomplish some things

_____ feel very nervous about being asked to accomplish things

_____ accomplish as much as anyone else

_____ do just about whatever I set out to do

If I could have a dream come true, it would be:

_____

Do you like to think about achieving great things:

_____ Yes

_____ No

What fears, if any, would hold you back from choosing Mary Kay as a part-time or full-time career at this time?

_____

What three work and/or people skills would you want to develop to reach a fuller success potential with your life?

_____

When it comes to life and work, how do you see yourself?

_____ an obsessive worker

_____ a good worker

_____ do as much as should be done

_____ a hard worker

_____ work hard sometimes

_____ try to choose jobs

What are some of your past achievements/successes that you are proud of in these areas?

Church related _____

Family related _____

Education/career related _____

From time to time the Director asks a small group of people selected from these interview sheets to get together with her and your Beauty Consultant. If your interview sheet is selected from the most outstanding candidates, would you like to meet with us over coffee?

_____ Yes

_____ No

Name _____ Date _____

Address _____ Zip _____

Home phone _____ Work phone _____

Best time of day to reach me is _____

Husband's name _____ Children? ____ Ages ____

My current occupation _____

What I like best about my current job _____

What I like least about my current job _____

Name of Beauty Consultant who talked to me _____

Training and Ongoing Meetings

Direct sales companies want you to enjoy the process of selling while making sales. They want you to succeed, and if you're of the mind, spirit, and constitution, they're happy to have you break and set company records. Most companies also help you as much as they can by providing training classes, most of which are arranged by the person who brought you into the company.

This is a business that depends on your being self-motivated much of the time and self-starting *all* of the time. You must know what to do and say in the field. You need a sense of optimism and ideas on how to perpetuate enthusiasm. Training sessions will provide many answers. Most of all, you'll need training to learn the essentials of product sales and demonstration, how to handle objections, make appointments, and recruit. And there are always many helping hands who serve as a support system.

You'll also be encouraged to get experience immediately. Anyone wishing to succeed will get to training sessions and attend weekly or bi-weekly sales meetings. You'll be sharing sales problems and triumphs with other salespeople and find the support you need as you accumulate experience. Among the benefits of training sessions is the knowledge that salespeople aren't born—they're made.

Even Sylvia Wolfe, Amway diamond direct distributor in Alaska, who did not have the benefit of training sessions and weekly sales meetings when she started, made this an essential part of her job despite the lack of a support system. "I didn't know how to sell and had no one to train me, but I stood in front of a mirror and said my speech about the products until I sounded pretty good," she says. "Then when I got to love the business and believe in it, I took classes on sales and business management. I was the first woman in Alaska to take the Dale Carnegie course, and I did a lot of reading on sales and personal growth."

Her commitment to success wasn't hindered by her isolation in small-town Palmer, Alaska—she created her own "training" from knowledgeable sources. Now with a large support system, Sylvia runs weekly sales meetings with "a bit of technique and a lot of motivation. Once a month, we meet to discuss business basics for new people and periodically, we have seminars." Twenty-one years later, Sylvia still finds inspiration and information at these meetings.

You'll benefit from two different kinds of meetings: 1) *Sales* meetings serve the purpose of weekly information exchange and motivation on an ongoing basis. (After all my experience and success, I still attend meetings frequently to be restimulated and resold on the career.) 2) *Training* meetings are geared specifically to people just coming into the business. They are a *must*—you learn the most effective techniques for selling *your* product and recruiting others into the company.

Training, then, provides the basics while sales meetings—preferably on a regular basis—establish a society of colleagues to learn from, to teach and to share your experiences with. Take advantage of what the company has to offer and . . . *be trained!*

III

Getting It All Together

Motivation and Goals

Don Bosson, a top division manager based in Joliet, Illinois and number one in the Fuller Brush company, is the quintessential committed salesman with strong values and valuable ideas about how to succeed in sales. He's been with the Fuller Brush company for nearly thirty years after a brief career as a luncheonette manager for W. T. Grant. He found his way to sales serendipitously.

"A friend told me he was selling for Fuller Brush and that it was a great thing to do. I thought I'd take a look at the business," he explained. "Since it was okay with the company for me to go out in the field with my friend, I did, and that clinched it. He was so *bad*—he did *everything* badly—that I thought, if this guy can make money selling door-to-door, so can I. As it turned out, I joined the company and he quit two months later."

Don excelled at sales and was promoted to field manager after two years, where he mostly recruited dealers. "At that time, twenty-four years ago, we just looked for men who wanted full-time sales jobs. It was company policy. Now that's all changed. We have mostly part-timers, and both men and women."

Over the years, he moved up to the top slot with Fuller Brush. What does he have that's special? How did he do it? What keeps him motivated? "It takes drive and desire. That's the start. You have to want to excel," he said. "When you excel, you think in terms of being a leader, not a follower. And if you want to be a leader, you'll be willing to put the effort forward that's good old-fashioned drive, to compete and be number one," he told me.

Don firmly believes that being a self-starter is "a must" in direct sales. However, many people will disagree with him. Though it's an asset to be a self-starter, many are not. They get their "push" through motivation by talking to or learning from others. Don felt differently and it worked for him. He advises, "Don't wait for someone to show you how to do anything. Just go and do it! Learn from your mistakes, but do it. Then do your best. It doesn't matter if you want the excitement that comes from the money or moving ahead. Take a chance on yourself."

These days, he's at his office at five-thirty or six in the morning, often putting in an eleven- or twelve-hour day. Don has made a lifetime commitment to his career, getting satisfaction from his achievements while still setting and meeting new goals.

Don and other outstanding direct sellers share an understanding of the qualities it take to achieve: persistence, energy, enthusiasm, goal-setting, and being self-starting. No one has actually come up with a formula describing the ideally successful salesperson. The formula will always vary because each one of us is unique—not only in terms of our strengths and weaknesses, but because of timing, location, and what we want. Also, we all don't aspire to being number one or number ten (or even number one hundred) in a company.

But *why* we want to achieve is another matter—and an individual one. Many of us need and crave recognition, and approval. Others are content with the more tangible rewards—high income, jewelry, cars, overseas trips—and might even shy away from public attention. Still others labor long and hard working for work's sake—they're intimately involved in being productive, needing to accomplish as much as they can in a lifetime. And yet others appreciate and enjoy dollops of each—a little recognition, some money, the pleasure of spending a day doing what one *likes*.

But anyone who has done well in this business did so with some measure of *self-esteem, self-motivation, the motivating spirit of others*, and *goal-setting*. These four qualities, to me, are the keys to success in this business, and a wise practitioner makes use of these basic principles right from the very first day.

Self-esteem and Self-motivation

The day you sign up with a direct sales company, you're automatically an entrepreneur. This means you are on your own, running your own "shop" in the manner that suits you best. It will operate by your own set of rules and goal-setting strategies, and of course there'll be changes to deal with and information to decipher. Each day will call for *effort* to keep going, especially when things look confusing or bleak. When you're an entrepreneur, you clock in and out at your chosen hours and your company operates almost entirely on *your own steam*! No boss will check up on you, there's no traveling to an office, and there's no guaranteed check on Fridays. The company you build at your desk reflects who you are and how you think. You decide the limits and how much money you'll earn. You've got to be *motivated*!

As in any business, you'll also hit spots of confusion, suffer a setback or two, and hopefully triumph over most of them. With experience, you'll begin to create order out of disorder—and smile when you realize how simple it really is. Rather than give up during the rougher times, you'll have the courage to go on and the smarts to seek guidance.

What does being an entrepreneur really entail?

When you're an entrepreneur, you'll be taking a number of risks. Risk taking may reward you with *success* when your efforts pay off. But taking risks can also bring rejection, teasing, and discouragement. In tougher times, you must call on your stronger self, shrug off negativity, and believe you're worthy and that what you're doing is worthwhile. I bring this point up again because it's so critical to winning in sales— you've got to roll with the punches and be guided by the force of your high *self-esteem*!

Surprisingly, many people think their self-esteem is *lower* than it is. I've listened to thousands of stories over the years of successful women and men who joined the sales business originally believing they'd fail. Barbara Hammond, the Home Interiors vice president mentioned earlier, told me, "Sometimes I meet women who've signed up with us and I discover that we are the *only ones* to have ever encouraged them to achieve something for themselves," she said. "I found there are so few women who *believe* in themselves, or think they even *have* potential."

Barbara and I, and so many other people like us who not only recruit but spend a lot of time giving speeches, running meetings, and motivating others have pretty much come to a similar conclusion: The reasons people give for lack of confidence have a common thread: Their abilities and limitations had been defined by relatives, friends, teachers, and bosses. Those limitations usually were restricting—No! You can't do this. No! No one in our family ever did that. No! You've got to ask me first before you make a decision. No! What makes you think you can do anything right? or a version of, "Your sister could probably do it well, but not you!" Negative reinforcement held them back for a long time, and didn't allow for much self-expression or fun. But the people who succeeded had their own spark, nevertheless, ignited by an idea—selling, starting small, but selling.

Psychologists know the power of praise and positive reinforcement, and every day, there are exotic laboratory experiments to demonstrate how suggestible we are to another's influence. Negative suggestions are defeating. That's all there is to know about that. Positive influence is enriching. That's what you need. You'll not only move further ahead with *praise* (self-directed or from others) but you'll work harder for the greater rewards it brings. A little success proves you *can* be successful.

Life offers us gifts and blights, surprises and routine—it's all part of a normal day. When you begin a business, you'll go through days of extreme highs and lows, days when you feel unsettled or ecstatic. Let it happen. On low days, don't give up. Hang in! Tell yourself that you learned something today, that you're okay, and tomorrow you'll start over, *still* okay.

I must emphasize this: *tell yourself that you are okay, not only when you triumph, but at the more vulnerable moments when you miss your mark.* You need to praise yourself in some way every day and reinforce the belief within yourself that you *are* okay. This "self talk" has helped me in my life—I know what an influence it can have.

Just recently, I discovered a book that clarified this idea for me better than all others I'd read in the past. It's called *What To Say When You Talk To Yourself* by Shad Helmstetter, Ph.D. The author explains first how our minds work—that is, just like computers. He writes: "The brain simply believes what you tell it most. And what you tell it about you, it will create. It has no choice." How simple it sounds—program a computer with a set of commands, and it *must* follow them because it knows no other way. Program your mind with a "set of commands" ("I can do this . . . I am worthy of a better life . . . I am a caring person . . ." and so on), and *that* will determine the shape of whatever life you choose. So if you remind yourself every day what a special person you are and that *you are capable*, you will be! Create this for yourself.

Self-esteem grows, gets stronger with each tiny step forward—one sale, one encouraging call, one sales meeting where you share your thoughts with others. These are the strengtheners of high self-esteem. Give yourself the opportunity to prove what you can do for yourself. Everything else will take care of itself.

Success in sales starts with *you*. No one is going to stand at your desk and set limits for you. If it's necessary for you, put up a sign on your desk that says, "If it's to be, it's up to me." Every day that you're in the business, you must make a choice to move forward and give up any excuses, habits, or thoughts that slow you down. Nothing leads to inertia faster than vivid and emotion-loaded fantasies about how you're going to fail. Lack of energy also leads to lack of interest. Soon enough, you're tired before the day begins. Excuses mount up one by one until they're a burden on the business They may even sound *real* to you, but usually excuses are given too much weight. They pave the way toward destroying a business and a career, often prematurely. Do these excuses sound familiar:

◆ No one's going to buy this product from me.

◆ I don't have the right clothes (looks, temperament) for this business, anyway.

◆ I'm too shy. Why did I let someone talk me into this?

◆ Life is already too much of a struggle. Why add to it by going into business?

Become conscious of these excuses and how they can begin to run your business instead of you being in charge. When you choose this career, you must give up self-defeating excuses one by one. Be aware that you're making them or finding busy work to keep you from devoting a fixed amount of time to your business. Every day you'll need to trim back the negativity. Try not to even think in terms of failure, if you can. Call it *experience*. You'll make mistakes, but make those mistakes count!

Most of us have tricks to get motivated and maintain enthusiasm. Usually our needs change as the business grows, and so, too, does our motivation and enthusiasm soar or falter. I am reminded of two interesting stories here on how to keep going.

Success is a personal matter. It's not only measured in terms of income and rewards—jewelry, furs, cars—but accomplishment and personal satisfaction. Marge Duenow, a Beauty Consultant with Mary Kay, is, at fifty-two, an interesting story of a woman who changed occupations in her late forties and far exceeded her notions of how much she'd accomplish. Marge saw herself as a woman who'd stay at a desk job forever and never stretch beyond that. With some success selling, her confidence in herself began growing. She did it this way:

"I was a medical secretary for seventeen years," Marge told me from her Glencoe, Minnesota, home, "for the head of a department. Then I worked for a surgeon for five years, sitting at a desk with earphones hanging from my ears, day in and day out." The routine began to get to her.

"One day one of my daughters asked me to get a few people together for a Mary Kay skin care class. I had no idea what it was or why I'd want to hostess a class, but I did," Marge said. She liked the company, the marketing plan, and the "extras" awarded for excellence—and she signed up.

Marge kept her job, working a forty-hour week while booking skin care classes—earning more in three shows with Mary Kay than she did in weekly salary. "I had to look at where my future was going. It suddenly struck me that I didn't have a lot to show for nearly twenty-five years at a desk job. But something was happening to me, and it was the knowledge that I should stay with sales."

After six months with Mary Kay, Marge became "Queen of Sales" for her unit, still not sure if selling was right for her. Ironically, she became ill, left her job for a while, then she returned to it. "I sat at that desk, started doing the same old thing and thought, *why*? I told my boss, 'I cannot stay here. Why should I make $14 after two hours of work here instead of earning $200 in *one morning* selling or recruiting?' I finally had the confidence to say it all out loud.

"I felt good enough about myself right then to know I'd make it. There have been times when I wanted to quit, but I kept in there by setting goals. I *need to see ahead*. I have a picture of what I want, then I go for it. What motivates me is helping people feel good about themselves. I also love the rewards for hard work. My outlook has become so positive because of this company that I don't look back."

Marge has won, among other prizes, five fur coats in two

years, one accompanying a large diamond bumble bee pin for being number one in sales for the entire company. "I gave the coats to my daughters and said, 'Tell people your mother won these coats, and tell them how!'"

Setting Goals

Many of us in direct sales have succumbed to the fantasy now and then about "overnight" success. With such lofty dreams, we can neglect the long process of reaching that success—the hard work, planning, frustrations, the triumphs along the way. We'd like to believe the career we start one morning is, by five in the evening, making us millionaires. Fantasies sound good and are easy to contemplate. But in real life, setting (and reaching) goals can make fantasies come true.

Goal setting is not as complex as it may appear. Setting goals is a big part of managing your business and it's crucial to success. Without a goal, your business has no focus and you don't accomplish much. When you try to run your career without a long-range goal, you'll feel buffeted by life, never taking charge of your abilities or discovering your true potential. And a goal needs a time limit, because without a limit, a goal is just a wish. *Know where you're going and how long it will take to get there.*

When you know where you're going, next you'll have to break down the goal into small progressive steps. Bit by bit, all the details will fall into place, as you gain experience. And experience will show you that you must decide on a direction.

Because of the nature of goal setting in this business, you *can* learn about how it works—even in an unusually pressured situation. You can discover a resourcefulness about yourself that's almost as satisfying as meeting a goal. Margaret Leonard's story illustrates what I mean.

One afternoon, Margaret, a top director with Mary Kay, called and told me that she had added her figures up and found she was $10,000 shy of meeting her half-million dollar goal for that year. Margaret had two days to make the closing deadline for the company's records. This meant she had to locate customers who were ordering or reordering, and she had to recruit people who'd recruit people who'd place large orders. Considering the situation, Margaret only saw her $490,000 worth of work *stopping* her from getting the recognition she sought.

"I can't do it," she said, dejected. I told her, "You have knocked yourself out all year and you *cannot* give up now. Not with two days to go." Margaret said, "I knew you would tell me I could do it. But how?"

Margaret had this $10,000 sum looming before her. She panicked. My advice was to break the goal down into ten $1,000 pieces, then divide the $1,000 pieces into smaller amounts. The problem already was starting to look soluble. Focusing on each $1,000 chunk, Margaret thought about who had promised to place this $600 order or that $150 reorder; who had said she'd sign on but was waiting for a check, and which woman had said she knew someone who wanted to be recruited. Eventually, we got together a list of people whose business could add up to $10,000.

Margaret then had to get on the phone and help each one of these women help *her* meet this goal. Well, Margaret made it! And in just two days!

It would have been easy for her to quit and pull the covers over her head when it looked like she didn't have enough time. Calling me showed that she had a need to still reach this goal. I had to do what I could. It was worth my time (although

I did not receive any commission from her) and hers to break down an *overwhelming* goal into many different smaller segments, solve the problems involved with each segment, and then put the pieces back together again.

I honestly don't know of anyone who would voluntarily put herself in such a pressured situation, but sometimes it can creep up on you. Then, it's up to you to meet the challenge of time by applying energy and commitment to your goal.

Although this business has people who are usually supportive (there's always someone to encourage, console, teach, laugh, and cry with), it's *you* who must persevere and let others know you want to make it happen.

Goal setting is an individual process, and the specific ideas you have on making money are entirely unique to you. But let me reemphasize the power of motivation that comes from self-esteem, as well as from being a good friend to others in the business. When you're feeling low, dubious, exhausted, indecisive, or even placidly content with where you are, there's always someone to cheer you on through all the vicissitudes of the business or remind you of your achievements. It's comforting to gather support from people who *want* you to do well—who have an investment in being on your side. Sometimes, that connection is all you need to break through a barrier and realize the great joy of meeting a goal!

Your persistence in reaching your goals determines how well you do. You'll have to make adjustments as you go along, but be ready with your goals and let them be the boss you always wanted. Whether your goal is to be number one (as in Don Bosson's case with Fuller Brush) or to earn an extra five hundred a month, you've given yourself a shining star to follow until you reach your "destination."

Goals aren't mysterious or ominous things. They're approachable, and if you're honest with yourself, you can formulate them so they mean something. Goals must fit you. One size does not fit all! What are the right goals for you? Here are some general ideas on the matter—on how to make them work to produce higher income and a better life.

First, some pointers to help you personalize your goals. **Goals must be easy to believe.** They should make some *sense* in your scheme of things—and not be unreachable.

Lily Tomlin once had a character of hers say, "I always wanted to be somebody. Now I see I should have been more specific." It's funny, but wise, too. The speaker is someone who sets impractical goals, floating through life wishing too hard for things that may always be out of reach. People like her may even see themselves as champion salespeople, but they don't put in the time to learn what *makes* a champion in sales. If you allow yourself to be too vague, you could end up wandering from point to point, hoping to stumble on what's right by accident. **Be specific. A goal must be able to work and take you somewhere better.**

When you set your goals, understand that they will change, because *you* change as you grow and get involved in the business and so will your goals. You'll see what you can earn, how to increase your power, what you will need to meet a goal, or why you should change your goal entirely.

One primary goal may be to make a lot of money. *That's okay.* But it's best to understand the power of money and how to put money and money making in perspective.

You might have felt a little flutter when you read of the income-producing possibilities, especially in direct selling companies. But something else is bound to happen when you work in direct sales—you'll develop a sense of self-worth and accomplishment.

The idea of making good money will conjure images of how your life would change by measure. So be specific. Are you doing this to earn money so your children can have some extras in life? Is your goal to get involved in a profession where you can actually engineer personal and financial growth according to your own schedule? Do you want to contribute to paying off monthly bills and relieve a spouse from complete financial responsibility? If you examine what money does, you may find that it resolves the pressures surrounding many issues—the bottom line of which is, "*Can I afford it?*"

If you're joining the business for the money, start specifying the areas in your life that could be improved by more—and give it a number. How much would it take? Don't be vague. "A lot" doesn't mean much. Will $1,000 free you in some way? Would you feel more secure with another $10,000 in your savings account? Picture that money and connect to it. Think in progressive steps to get it.

Describe your goal. Picture your goal. Is it clear to you or fuzzy around the edges? Can you describe the beginning and the end, but falter when you have to give shape to the middle—the *core* that tells you how to achieve the goal itself? Write it all down in detail.

"To succeed, you must state a goal and go for it," suggests Nicky Lehman, a Portland, Oregon, super sales manager for Discovery Toys. Nicky has been with her company for five years, and she's had a meteoric rise. "At one time," she confessed, "I was actually proud that I'd never been to a Tupperware party. You could tell me about any direct sales company and I'd have a negative reaction. Then life changed for me and by a fluke, I wound up selling. Once I decided to turn it into an incredible adventure, I had to set goals for myself."

Nicky uses a technique that works for anyone with an honest desire to succeed—picturing herself as she wants to be and doing what is necessary to get there. "The key is to *visual-*

ize the goal—see, smell, and feel it. Make it real for yourself. Condition yourself to feel and accept that sense of achievement. The same thing happens when you make a sale. You can take yourself mentally through the process and feel positively about every step as if it were actually happening. Selling, then, becomes more natural, when you're face to face with a prospect. When you visualize yourself in a successful position, you can come to believe in yourself. It gives you the confidence to go on."

I never started out saying that I wanted to be number one in the company. As I reset each goal and got the recognition and financial rewards I wanted at each level, I developed greater self-confidence. When I decided to go for the top spot, I believed I could do it. I wanted this career to work for me for the rest of my life and I had to learn how to do it right. I wrote down how I thought I could get there step by step, and then I did it.

Reaching a goal in direct sales involves the following:

1) **Know your income goals:** Do you want to increase earnings by an extra $400 a month? Can you have regular meetings, parties, or one-to-one appointments to introduce others to the products? How many calls will you make a week? How much money will you invest in inventory? How many people will you recruit each month?

When you actually begin in direct sales, you'll have a much clearer idea of what to do and how long it will take to get your work done. You'll see how smooth goal setting can be.

"Sometimes, you can start out wanting nothing but pin money," said Camilla Kuhn, a Westville, New Jersey, district manager for Doncaster, "and before you know it, the money's $20,000 a year or more." Now fifty-two years old, Camilla originally just liked the idea of selling the kind of clothes she loves to wear and found she had fun doing it. She stayed with Doncaster, deciding to make it her career.

"Many of us entered the business with no real opinion of direct sales or knowledge of how much we could earn," she continued. "Since your hours are flexible to start, find out what you can do well and how to increase your earnings steadily. The best way: know your obligations to yourself and the company."

2) **State your goal to someone important.** Mary Kay Ash tells of how this step in goal setting made a big difference in her own rise to success. When she was new to direct sales and still a faltering and insecure salesperson with Stanley Home Products (Stanhome), she attended her first company "seminar." One subject discussed was stating your goal with the company. Each person in the audience was called upon to stand up and do so. Mary Kay was at the back of the room, listening attentively. When it was her time to state her goal, she walked down the aisle directly up to Mr. Beveridge, the president of the company, and said to him, "Next year, I'm going to be your Queen." He looked at her and said sincerely, "Somehow, I know you will!"

The point is: Mary Kay wanted to be honored the next year at Stanhome's seminar as the best, the "Queen." She told her goal to a person who would understand it—that is, someone who *was* a success and knew what it took to persist in this business. What mattered most, though, was that Mr. Beveridge knew that Mary Kay really meant what she said and he offered sincere words of encouragement to her. Those few words are inspiring and motivating. Find a role model within your direct sales company whom you can talk to, even briefly, and state your goal to him or her. I guarantee that you will be encouraged!

3) **Give yourself enough time to reach a goal:** When you

start working in direct sales and see the possibilities actually materialize, in your excitement you might list goals you want to accomplish within absolute time frames. You'll find that each company awards titles appropriate to different levels of production and income—you may start off as a "distributor" or "consultant." As your income increases, you may be eligible for "supervisor" or "sales manager," "director" or "division manager," and so on. Higher levels offer greater commissions and rewards or bonuses and you may want to reach these levels as fast as possible. You might slot one year for one title, or six months of hard work for another, and on and up the scale.

If you've got the fever to make it big, you should seek advice from an expert at your company on how to get where you want to go, and how long it will take. What will be expected of you? Can you reasonably hit your goal without rushing it or putting excessive pressure on yourself?

Each company establishes a policy about what is required for title change and with it, increased earnings. Most likely you'll have to fulfill a certain monthly sales minimum—for example, $3,000 or $3,500 a month in unit sales to be a manager or supervisor. Suppose you've now been told that, on the average, a beginning consultant needs about 12–18 months to reach a particular sales level. Decide how to do it.

Examine what you've done in the first *six months* and decide how to achieve your goal without straining. Will you need to devote more time to it each week? Do you need to recruit *new* people or more *enthusiastic* ones? Probably both. Once you get the feel of the business, it becomes important to devise a master plan as a tool to reach the goals you've set for yourself.

Women with young children can still reach their goals, but it may take them longer because of other demands on their time. I spent many years making a pie with one hand and setting up appointments with the other. The fact is that motherhood helps us master the art of multiple accomplishments out of necessity. I started my business when my children were all in their teens and time was tight. I had my business goal, though—and it mattered enough for me to *find* the time. When you're busy running a home, the steps you take forward may be tinier, but tiny steps ease you closer to your goals anyway! As the direction of your life shifts day to day, just steer toward your goal from another angle. Make your phone calls at night, rather than during "working hours" if that is what comes up for you. If need be, allow yourself to slow down your pace when caring for family business becomes the priority. In your heart you'll know the difference between making excuses and when there are real demands on your life. If that's the case, don't get frustrated because you're off schedule.

"We're pioneers of a sort in this business," said Sue Frederickson, a dynamic New Orleans-based manager for Discovery Toys, speaking of the force women with children have had upon the direct sales business. "We take care of each other and help each other get moving. Most of us have families and children and understand what it means to succeed and enjoy the rewards of a part-time career."

Sue, now 35, began her professional life as a teacher. A friend invited her to a demonstration of Discovery Toys, though she'd never considered selling them. "After listening for five minutes, I was sold! I loved the toys and bought the whole kit. That was 1981. That fall season I sold $10,000 worth of toys." Since then, Sue's moved up steadily in the company.

To reach her success, Sue formulated a personal theory that "anyone can win with three keys to success." The first is enthusiasm. "Talk about your product all the time," she advises, "and don't hesitate to recruit when you can. Just draw interest, and don't be pushy. Perseverance is second: There will always be days when you wonder if this career is worth anything. I think this is a universal feeling—everyone has thought this, no matter who. But you have to *hang in* there—during low times, slow seasons—overcoming doubts about yourself. And most important to me, conscientious goal setting. Set your sights, set up a structure. If it means more recruiting or more hours, decide how you'll do it day by day. You'll make it if you believe in yourself and your goal."

Be kind to yourself. If success is your plan, pat yourself on the back for doing even a little work—don't diminish your efforts just because you didn't meet an *ideal* timetable.

Make out a master plan that details your goals and how you envision meeting them within the first two or three years, and how to meet them realistically. The first twenty-four to thirty-six months are very important. This is where you'll develop expertise; expand your knowledge about selling, about the product, about dealing effectively with others; and become an entrepreneur as you set up working schedules and stick to them as closely as possible. You'll work hard these two to three years. But remember, though you may sometimes fall behind, at other moments, you'll surge ahead.

Some people become discouraged with the amount of money they've earned over the first two years and let all that effort go nowhere! They give up on themselves and a direct sales career when they just needed to take a breath, then keep going.

Draw up a realistic program for increasing income by "X" amount each year: Decide how much you'd like to earn within your first year. Perhaps an extra $200 for a period of three months, then up to $500 for six months more, then

$1,000 a month for the last three months of the year. A number of us meet such goals—and some far exceed it, but it always takes exceptional commitment, focus, ambition, and sales ability to do it. Recognizing the small successes helps us reach for more and greater goals. Remember, too, that recruiting others can increase your income tremendously, since you'll be earning a percentage on their sales. Try not to put off recruiting others and include it in your plan to increase income.

In most cases, you won't clear $12,000 or certainly $20,000 or more in the first year working part-time. You can, though, realistically make about $100–$150 per week when you start. That's pretty good! Remember: When you go into business for yourself—especially if it's for the first time—don't expect miracles. Be happy to start a second year after twelve exceptional months of learning, trial and error, perfecting sales approaches, adjusting schedules, figuring out the most expedient ways to fill orders, and so on. You'll be putting effort into building a career, and if you're smart, you'll accept the possible lower-than-anticipated profits at the end of the first year, knowing that all you can do is grow.

Invest in yourself that first year and try not to place too much emphasis on instant riches.

You can be a whiz at sales technique, go to training sessions and sales meetings on a regular basis, attend seminars and conventions, but without a specific *goal*, you will not succeed. Goals help you define what you want and give a name to your next destination. Few of us would consider packing the family in the car, backing down the driveway, and taking off for *anywhere*. Driving aimlessly is hardly considered a productive journey and conflicting opinions about where to go can make the trip an unpleasant one. The same issues hold true for your career. *Choose* the road you will take, know where it's going, and be alert for meeting new opportunities as you travel it step-by-step meeting your goals. Most of all, have a great time on the trip!

Putting Your Business Together

Direct sales relies on basics, such as dealing effectively with time management, learning the trade, working with others, and running a business. Since you'll most likely be working from home, your base of operations will have to function in an orderly and professional manner.

If you've never run a business from home before, you'll wonder how it's actually done . . . and sometimes, *where* it's done. Perhaps you are thinking about where your "office" would be physically located in your home. Be comforted to know that even if you live in a studio apartment, you can effectively arrange "office space." If you are lucky enough to have an extra room, alcove, or part of a finished basement, you're ahead of the game. And don't overlook a large *closet* either—I've met a number of resourceful salespeople who have converted one into a habitable, attractive, and credible work space!

When I started with Mary Kay, I immediately thought of

myself as a *businesswoman*—a professional. That meant I needed simple office materials, supplies, and organizational tools to help me run my business. Becoming a business-woman also demanded that I'd have to sit down and arrange an office in the space available and make it work best for me. I took my career seriously and I was in business to succeed. I'd have to remain motivated and educated. I couldn't go half-way, but do everything I could to make my work space and working attitude a powerful combination.

I started this way:

Time Management

There was a man named Ivy Lee who made a clever sug-gestion for his boss, Charles Schwab, that paid off in a num-ber of ways. He created a time-efficient office system that was pure and simple, so simple, in fact, that it appeared it could never work. But it did! Mr. Lee received something like $35,000 for his idea and it was this: If everyone wrote down the six most important things to do each day, and did them one by one, time would be better managed and more could be accomplished.

There's a lot of psychology involved in listing tasks, doing them, then crossing them off the list. Also a lot of satisfaction in knowing how much you really *are* capable of doing. At the end of the day, you can peruse the list and see what kind of shape your day was in. Then evaluate how long it took you to do one task or the other, and decide how to be more efficient.

In addition, list making helps you get right to the point, problem solve, and so forth, all by establishing priorities. Ac-tual performance may vary from task to task, but what mat-ters is that you identify your goals on a daily basis, and write them down. This is time management honed down to a fine art.

It's almost always better to start with the toughest, most *important* tasks and work your way through to the easier ones later in the day. This makes sense to me. You'll have to do the task anyway, so why not do it now! Don't overload the list, confuse yourself, or try to overachieve. Keep your lists manageable and realistic. That way, you *will* succeed.

A second crucial link to time management is this: Never handle a piece of paper more than once if you can help it. Mary Kay herself once gave me this advice, and I've followed it as conscientiously as I could over the years. It's also advice given by time-management experts, and those of us in business know what it can mean in getting through the day. I've discovered, and so will you, that sometimes a piece of paper needn't be filed and given undue importance, but tossed out. If *in doubt, then toss it out*! You can lose yourself in mountains of notices, newsletters, greeting cards, duplicates and triplicates of receipts, letters, memos, and bills, and never see the light of day. File only that which is critical to keep—order forms, inventory orders, information about your recruits, commission schedules.

Time management also refers to making time work for you. One of the bigger problems people have who run a business from home is keeping *structure* to the day. Those who get up each morning to an alarm, leave the house to get to a job, work, then come back home, pretty much have the day regulated for them by employers. Not so with the direct sales entrepreneurs working from home. When you are on your own, it's very tempting to get up later (if you have no children or family member who need tending to) and do chores other than those for business. The attitude may be, "Oh, I have all day. I can do it later." It can become a *habit* to spend time doing nothing productive for your business unless you standardize your day to discipline yourself. Here's what I suggest:

Each Sunday night (if that is best for you) set up a weekly schedule, broken down by day, and then by hours within those days. Construct a picture of a real work week ahead for yourself and follow it as best you can. This time-management tip is one that is highly recommended by Sue Frederickson, a dynamic saleswoman with Discovery Toys. A mother of three small children, Sue keeps to her list of priorities, but emphasizes "you must keep business hours when you work at home. Let everyone know what your hours are and ask people to *honor* your schedule," she told me. "Unless you set up office hours, you'll get caught and find ways to frazzle yourself out. It's so easy to get off the track and deal with your family's needs first, or cut a business phone call short when you should really stay on."

Since one of the benefits of direct sales *is* setting your own hours, you don't want to let things get out of control so that you feel one responsibility (your family) is infringing on the other (your business), or vice versa. Barbara DerHohannesian, a key coordinator for Shaklee, based in Wellesley Hills, Massachusetts, summed up what pleases her most about her home-based business, now in its fifteenth year: "The *flexibility* to be with my family and succeed in business at the same time." Barbara specializes in helping others develop communication and leadership skills, along with guiding them in the interrelated time and personal-life management. (Many of us in direct sales ardently believe that if you can organize your work life so it's productive, it can have a beneficial effect on your personal life—for one, because your feelings of self-esteem go up!)

Now a single parent of three daughters, Barbara has always appreciated the "flex time" of running a business from home. "Not only have I been able to build a business," she said, "but it's also been good for my daughters to see that a woman can succeed. They see me in action, they know how I set goals and meet them. I've immersed myself totally in my business, knowing that I'm the only one who can make it happen. Because of Shaklee, though, I've had the chance to work and still be there for my family when they needed me."

Beyond the benefits of flexible time for business and family—and actually setting a good example for your children—there are other points to keep in mind to get the most from your day:

◆ Keep tasks within a time frame. Without a deadline, you may easily become distracted, discouraged, or overenthusiastic. Give yourself only so much time to do the job and then stop.

◆ Politely get chatty friends off the phone during business hours by saying, "Let me call you back later," or tell your caller that you're in a business meeting and can't talk now.

◆ Do you function best in the early morning? Late day? Then it makes sense to do your most creative thinking, more detailed work, or physically demanding chores while your metabolism is at its strongest. Do some clever shifting around of appointments or tasks to best suit your nighttime or morning personality. If you are a morning person (or even if you're not), try arising at 5:00 A.M. or 6:00 A.M. to see how much more you can accomplish before 9:00 A.M. You will be amazed.

♦ Some perfectionists might say that shortcuts short-change us, but if you're running a family and a business from home, most shortcuts are well worth the price. As your business becomes more active, think about ways to get from point A to point D without stopping at points B and C. Your time is valuable.

Once you think in terms of *organization* and *priorities* you'll be way ahead of the game.

Now, let's organize your office.

Putting Your Office Together

If you approach your "office" in the most professional manner, you can't lose. No more piles, just files. Think *order*. Once you organize whatever space can function as your office, you'll begin to see a sense of purpose take shape. Organization helps you run on the right track. Not only does it motivate you to work, it creates tangible evidence of your dedication that begins the moment your office is set up.

Setting Up

You'll need an area that can contain a desk or small table (my choice), a phone, some wall space for a bulletin board (to post memos, notices, and pictures of what you'd like to win or buy). You'll also need a filing cabinet or cardboard filing system to start.

Can you appropriate an entire room for your office? This is a luxury. But if you're like most of us, you'll do some creative juggling to set up a permanent space. You'll want to ease into your business day with as little readjustment as possible. Reserve a desk or table that will be solely your business hotline center that no one else may use. The same goes for the wall space around one side of the desk; that's for the bulletin board.

You'll do best with a phone number that's yours alone. This is important to your business. Call the phone company and order a second listing in your name, at your residence. A good deal of business is transacted by phone. Nothing's more unnerving than having to bargain with someone who's using the only phone in the house so you can take an order or speak to a potential recruit. When you've got two phones at your disposal, you can be more efficient.

If you decide not to have a phone number separate from the family's, that's okay. But remember this: People are more likely to find you if you're listed. In most direct sales companies, you can have a yellow pages (or white pages) listing when you have reached *managerial* level. For example, I can be listed under the *Mary Kay* heading in the phone book, along with other Mary Kay people who have qualified themselves by fulfilling a requirement from the company. As we mentioned earlier, each company will have a different qualification for "manager" or "supervisor"—depending on the number of the recruits you've brought in, your retail sales figures, or both. If you do reach managerial level, it is your *option* to pay for and have a listing of your name under the company heading. Check with your company on its policy for phone book listings.

In addition, get an answering machine to handle calls when you're not in. This is much more professional than having your child (or other relative) taking messages, not to mention the possibility that they might forget to leave you an important message. If you're worrying about the extra cost of another phone, remember that if you use it for business, most of the charges are tax deductible.

Keep an Updated Card File or Address Book

When you're doing business, you need to find the people who contribute to it. Be sure you have the address and phone number of each client and recruit you work with, all the people you'd eventually like to contact for more business, and for temporary office help, a stationery store, typewriter repair shop, and so on.

Display Your Product

Display your wares if you've got the space. Since you're making money by selling products, you should want others to see what you're selling. Showcases or bookcase-size cabinets aren't necessary, nor is putting out every product in your line. But let everyone know you're seriously in business by either lining up your products on a bathroom shelf or kitchen shelves (if you're in cosmetics or household products) or in small attractive boxes if you're a jewelry seller. Wear what you're selling, if that's appropriate to the occasion, or hang a few items on padded hangers on the outside of bedroom closet doors. If you really have no room for display, leave your company's pamphlets, annual reports, magazines, or pictures of the products on a desk or tabletop. You'll probably be entertaining guests a few times a month and talking about your business. Since we know visuals help, people may indulge in impulse buying or even sign up to work with you simply by seeing your products displayed.

Simple Organizational Systems

To me, nothing's more perfect an organizer than the homely file folder. My file system is pretty much a conventional system, with all folders kept in alphabetical and month-by-month order. There are so many streamlining ideas to keep business accounts, especially now with high-tech computers at our command. As your business grows, you'll discover the best system and software for your purposes, your kind of product, and the projected volume of your business.

Finances

No business can function without a few financial ground rules. For a direct sales operation, you'll need to spend some money to earn some back. My suggestion is to start this way: If you have a joint checking account with your spouse, or even if you have your own account, open a second one under your name, too. Any bank will tell you what's required for a "special" checking account—and it's most likely a small expense for you.

This checking account should be used entirely for business. It will reflect some of the money you'll be depositing from profits and allow you to pay your expenses, such as, needed inventory. If you need cash to buy stationery or stamps, pay for photocopying services or for any item that involves selling your product, just write out a check to "cash." Keep track of what you do with your business money in a small book you label "cash outlay." Keep track of where your profits are going and establish good records for tax purposes. Taxes is no one's favorite subject . . . but things can work out better than you thought in this matter. Here's an overview of why you may actually enjoy knowing what the IRS will allow you if you run a business from home.

Tax Benefits: How To Keep More of the Money You Earn

There are many benefits that come with a career in selling. And there is one benefit that's dear to every direct seller's heart—a wide range of tax breaks for operating a business from your home. I recommend that you mention this to any possible recruit. Before I began selling Mary Kay, I was drawing a number of taxed salaries—from my TV show, modeling, speaking to women's clubs, and so on, and I had no idea what an exceptional "perk" these tax breaks could be.

Without showing elaborate tax forms charting inflation rates vis-à-vis the shrinking dollar, I'll describe some bottom-line information about the advantages of a home business. Here's how it works.

A few years ago, Congress enacted some laws to help businesses, doing so to create an "economic recovery." These "incentives" were tax breaks. In other words, *deductions*.

In my case, getting these tax breaks was an *additional* incentive for me to start in direct sales. At first, the list of deductions sounded too good to be true, but when I considered it in terms of running a small business, it made perfect sense. All direct salespeople who *can*, take these deductions.

We live in a free enterprise system, where we work, invest, spend, and save money. In this system, we can be employed by big business or go into business for ourselves. By doing so, we are—as entrepreneurs—actually encouraged and supported by some laws. Why? When we go into business, we are taking a chance—risking something for eventual gain—and by doing so, creating capital, providing employment, and participating in and stimulating the economy.

I used to believe that nothing could be more secure than getting paid a salary. You know the feeling: Here's this amount of money at the end of the week or the end of the month or the end of a free-lance job. The government, predictably, is happy to take its share in withholding taxes, while the state and local levels ask for a cut, too. In many cases, a worker may be paying twenty-five to sixty percent of his (or her) weekly salary to taxes, depending on the salary and number of dependents.

Going into business for yourself, though, puts you in a different category. This is the difference between you the salaried worker and you the entrepreneur. You the worker are someone who is on salary at a company—and that company must pay health benefits, retirement, and such. You may be productive, but you are *costing* them income, unless you are at a high enough executive level where you actually *produce* income for them. But when you're an entrepreneur, at your desk with your phone and your folders and your calendar, the government is willing to give you a break so you can hopefully stay in business and help stimulate the economy.

By becoming a direct sales person working at home, you put yourself in the same position, though on a lesser scale, as any major corporation in the country. You, too, can take similar tax deductions. For example, when you work for a corporation, you could have the "perk" of an expense account. On a specified day, according to the company's schedule, you'll be expected to tally up your expenses—lunches, taxis, and so on—and put in a voucher for the total sum. The company then issues you a check for that amount. They're reimbursing you for entertainment or travel which you did on behalf of company business. The company reimburses you for an economically sound reason. They figure, "Let's pay back Miss Green for her traveling expenses to meet a prospective client." Why? The company will then use your voucher as one of their legitimate deductions when it's tax time.

As an entrepreneur, you may not get quite the scope of tax breaks as a huge company, but the ones you get *count*! Will you be traveling to see a retail customer or to recruit? I've taken many four- and five-hour drives to meet with potential recruits and people already working for Mary Kay. Gas, oil, and car depreciation are valid deductions. Will you be entertaining those same customers or prospective recruits at a brunch or dinner? These are deductible expenses for your business.

Becoming a direct salesperson working from home makes you a businessperson with the identical goals, theoretically, as a giant corporation. The goals are to make a profit, stay in business, keep growing. By doing what they do, you can declare deductions similar to theirs.

The government likes to know you're in business with the *intent*—and that's the key word—with the *intent* to make a profit. Anyone going into business should know that the first year or so in most cases, won't be unusually exceptional. But even though you've invested very little in your inventory, you may, because of a variety of circumstances, make a minimal kind of profit during your first few years. Let's say you earned three or four thousand dollars a year from working part-time at home in your own business. You'd have many more deductions, and therefore an opportunity to keep more of that money, than if you'd earned three or four thousand dollars in salary.

The home business tax breaks are *many* and you'll need the advice of an accountant to sort them all out when it's time to file your returns. Meanwhile, here's a sampling of what a direct sales business can do for you. Although the numbers will be different by the time you read this book (because of the new tax laws), the following should give you a good idea of how running a business from home may be profitable:

Deductions and Benefits Involving Your Spouse and Children

These numbers may help clarify what you're paying out in taxes if you're married and filing a joint tax return.

An average couple, paying standard income taxes, may take such valid tax deductions as medical expenses and charitable contributions. But basic expenses such as rent, telephone, and so on *cannot* usually be considered deductible under typical conditions. However, if one or both have jobs and *also* start a direct sales business—a business that will provide a second source of income—this couple is then eligible for a variety of different and legal deductions. A percentage of your total yearly rent and mortgage payments is among them. Because of those deductions, the couple may get to keep more money and put more money back into the business to encourage its growth.

These deductions are just one incentive for married couples to start a direct sales business. Another is "retirement." Many salaried people have begun putting away $2,000 each year in an Individual Retirement Account (IRA), which has been non-taxable up to now.* The self-employed may also have a Keogh Plan—a special tax shelter for the self-employed. A few years ago, the maximum you could deposit

---

*Please check with your accountant regarding IRA changes in the new tax law of 1986.

in your Keogh per year was 15 percent of your income or $15,000, whichever was higher. The sum has gone up to $30,000—a terrific opportunity for direct sales entrepreneurs to shelter a large percentage of their incomes.

If you are the parent of a typical child, you'll be dipping into your handbag more times per day than you'd care to count. Children need new sneakers, want extra spending money or a computerized toy, need school uniforms, want to go to the movies and out for dinner, need lunch money, want their ears pierced. What if it's tough for you to meet all those financial demands?

A teenage child with some resourcefulness may go out and get a part-time job. Younger children can also pick up the odd job, but it's a bit harder for the ten- or twelve-year-old to rely on steady income on a part-time basis coming in every week. One solution:

With a direct sales home business, your children can work for you in your company. The government allows each of them to earn a certain amount per year without filing a tax return. If you had a big business, with a large volume of products going in and out, you could decide to pay a younger child $10 a week for a few hours of doing simple jobs like stamping envelopes. Pay your child by check. At the end of the year, you can deduct all those checks as expenses paid out for an assistant. If you have a teenager, you can delegate more responsibility to him or her—answering the phone, taking orders and more. This child can earn $50 or so a week for legitimate office work. These salaries are deductible for you and the children are learning to contribute to their own lives by working . . . while helping you out and earning money. You're not just giving them allowances.

Children can generally do the following for a direct selling business: pack boxes, ship out packages, stamp envelopes and flyers, deliver products, set up a room for a meeting, clean it up before guests arrive, take orders by phone, even man the phones if you're out of the office for the day or traveling for the week.

Most important in hiring a child is to keep the salary level in balance with the size of your business and the actual work load.

Cars and Travel

The IRS is very fussy about the deductions you'll want to take for using your car for business, so always keep receipts. If you use your car exclusively in your business or work, you may deduct all of the cost of its operation. The deductible items include the cost of gas, oil, tires, repairs, insurance, depreciation, interest to buy the car, taxes, licenses, garage rent, parking fees, tolls, and so on. You'll want to keep fastidious records about where you went, on what day, to see whom, and why. Keep a travel diary, and note the mileage, for example, if you're going either to meet customers or recruits, or even if you are attending a seminar related to improving your business.

And now for the trip itself: as a self-employed person, you can deduct all travel-related expenses—motels, hotels, meals. If you visit one of your distributors in another state and take your younger sister along for the ride, you can deduct your portion of the trip, but not hers. Keep separate receipts. (Of course, if your sister sells, too, then the whole trip is deductible. For the same reason, you may want to sign her up, so that any calls or visits to her can be on business, too.)

If you have a second home—one you own—and do business from there sometime during the year, you can deduct all travel-related expenses to and from it.

Gifts

You can legally write off $25 worth of gifts for each person who is a customer of yours, or, in fact, to anyone you do business with. That makes gift giving doubly nice. It's a huge expense, for example, at Christmas to buy so many presents for the people who've been your loyal customers and/or supportive recruits and associates. Big business usually does it another way, with Christmas bonuses and presents like boxes of imported chocolate or twelve-year-old Scotch. A friend received a wonderful glass bowl from Tiffany's for Christmas from her boss—a lovely present and she was touched. Yes, her boss was thoughtful and generous, but so too was he counting that Tiffany's receipt in his gift deductions.

You can too.

At-home Tax Breaks

Remember this: ''double-A'' deductions. They can mean a lot to you when doing your tax planning for your home business. Because you operate a business from your home, you're eligible to deduct certain expenses if they're related to running and maintaining that at-home office. Keep scrupulous accounts and seek the advice of an accountant before filing, to be sure you fulfill all requirements for the IRS.

The home-office deductions are numerous—and begin with the actual room itself. If you are using an entire room for an office, there should be no problem; when using a *portion* of the room, the IRS is happier to know there's a partition set up to separate living quarters from actual office space. If you've got a big business and use your finished basement or other room for business entertaining, storage of your products, conferences, or even small seminars, this area qualifies, too, as a deduction. In all, you can deduct from 20 to about 50 percent or so of your monthly rent (or mortgage or maintenance costs), depending on the size of the office space as a percentage of the entire house. Fuel, electricity, even a portion of the grocery bill can be deducted if you're doing entertaining for business at home. (You can also deduct up to 25 percent of *second home* costs, as of this writing, including deductions for entertaining, fuel, and so on.)

These bills are ones you'd have to pay, regardless of whether you've got a flourishing business at home or not. With the addition of a home office, expenses are converted to deductions.

The bigger your business, the more you can include expenses related to improving your property—when they involve areas that would be used for business, that is. For example, you may be able to deduct landscaping your property, or putting in a pool (you must show evidence that you transacted business poolside), and redecorating and renovating the room or rooms you use for offices. But until you reach these levels of prosperity, you can take deductions for some of the basics in running the office itself:

◆ **The phone:** the basic charge per month is deductible along with the number of calls apportioned to business (as opposed to personal calls). This is if you're using the family phone. A business phone, along with all your long distance calls meant for business, is 100 percent deductible.

◆ **Telephone answering machine and typewriter:** both can be depreciated over a number of years—25 percent per year is typical.

♦ **Office supplies:** any stationery, business cards, stamps, paper clips, stapler, pens, manila folders, clipboards—all of these are totally deductible. Save every receipt—even one from a photocopy service for one letter.

As you set up your business and make it work, put income back into it or invest, you'll discover additional deductions. The more involved you become in the business—making it grow slowly from a sideline, extra-income producer to a full-time opportunity—the more the business will dictate your lifestyle. Over the years, you can be living well, but paying much less tax than if you were making an equivalent amount at a salaried job.

Direct sales is an exciting business opportunity, and the tax breaks will not usually be the prime incentive for starting out. But even though taxes or retirement benefits aren't of primary consideration in choosing a career, it's worth your attention in terms of savings and income for the future. Choose your company well, and examine all the benefits available to get the most from the business you'll be creating!

A Final Thought

Funny thing about the future. We begin with an idea of what our lives will be like and sometimes along the way, there's a turnaround—a surprise in self-discovery that takes us down an unexpected path. I started out with the idea of achieving at something while doing my best. I found my calling in sales and I built a life that's fulfilling and still challenging.

I'm representative in many ways of many women. I've encountered most of the problems that women face, particularly the dual responsibility of building a career while caring for a family. For me, direct selling was the answer to balancing my life between business and family.

One last word of advice . . .

When you start your business, stay cool. Be flexible. Keep your sense of humor. Ultimately, be willing to allow yourself a number of failures and setbacks. Be kind to yourself when they happen . . . and don't lose faith! Count on yourself and your abilities and *be there* with your energy and commitment 100 percent!

I offer all my warmest wishes to you and expect that when you start in direct sales, you'll understand why I think this is *the* business for the future . . . and I hope, for you, too. I look forward to hearing about you in the business very soon.

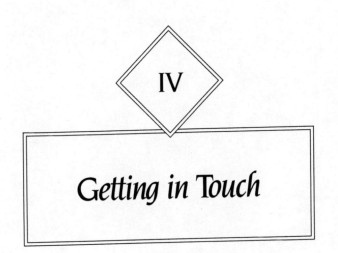

IV

Getting in Touch

Direct Sales
Companies

On the following pages, you'll find a fairly comprehensive list of direct sales companies. Nearly all of them belong to the industry group, the Direct Selling Association in Washington, D.C. To get more information about these companies, you may contact the association at 1730 M Street NW, Washington, D.C. 20036 (202-293-5760) or write directly to the company that interests you.

If you have difficulty contacting any of these companies at the listed addresses (which were accurate as this book went to press), please contact the Direct Selling Association.

1. ACT II JEWELRY, INC.
101 Leland Court
Bensenville, IL 60106
312-860-3323
(Jewelry—fashion & fine)

2. ALCAS CUTLERY CORP.
1116 East State Street
P.O. Box 810
Olean, NY 14760-0810
716-372-3111
(Cutlery/cookware/
tableware)

3. ALFA METALCRAFT
      CORP. OF AMERICA
   7970 Bayberry Road
   Suite 10
   Jacksonville, FL 32216
      904-731-8200
   (Cookware)

4. AMERICA'S
      BUYERS, INC.
   339 East 16 Street
   Holland, MI 49423
      616-392-7141
   (Buyer's club)

5. AMERICAN DREAM
      INTERNATIONAL, INC.
   8500 Doe Avenue
   Visalia, CA 93291
      209-651-3700
   (Cosmetics—skin/hair
      & health)

6. JOHN AMICO
      COSMETICS, INC.
   7327 West 90 Street
   Bridgeview, IL 60455
      312-430-2552
   (Cosmetics & skin care)

7. AMWAY CORPORATION
   7575 East Fulton Road
   Ada, MI 49355
      616-676-6000
   (Household/personal
      care/home care/
      nutritional products/
      catalog)

8. ARBONNE
      INTERNATIONAL, INC.
   22541 Aspen Drive
   El Toro, CA 92630
      714-770-2610
   (Cosmetics/skin care)

9. AUBREY McDONALD
      CREATIONS, INC.
   565 Wolf Ledges
      Parkway
   Akron, OH 44311
      216-376-4122
   (Jewelry—costume)

10. AVACARE, INC.
    9200 Carpenter Freeway
    Dallas, TX 75247
       214-638-7686
    (Cosmetics—skin, hair &
       health care products)

11. AVON PRODUCTS, INC.
    9 West 57 Street
    New York, NY 10019
       212-546-8500
    (Cosmetics/jewelry)

12. BASKET PEOPLE HOME
       PARTIES, LTD.
    P.O. Box 67
    Taftville, CT 06380
       203-886-1404
    (Decorative accessories/
       wicker products)

13. BEAUTICONTROL, INC.
    3311-400 Boyington
    P.O. Box 815189
    Carrollton, TX
       75381–5189
       214-458-0601
    (Cosmetics)

14. BETTER LIVING
       PRODUCTS, INC.
    600 Busse Road
    Elk Grove Village, IL
       60007
       312-956-0900
    (Household/nutritional/
       personal care
       products)

15. BRITE MUSIC
       ENTERPRISES, INC.
    3357 South 2300 East
    Box 9191
    Salt Lake City, UT 84109
       801-487-5891
    (Children's song books/
       cassettes/records)

16. THE BRON-SHOE
       COMPANY
    1313 Alum Creek Drive
    Columbus, OH 43209
       614-252-0967
    (Baby shoe bronzing)

17. CAMEO
       COUTURES, INC.
    9004 Ambassador Row
    Dallas, TX 75247

       214-631-4860
    (Clothing/lingerie/bras/
       loungewear)

18. CATTANI CALIFORNIA
    5510 Cleon Avenue
       North
    North Hollywood, CA
       91609
       818-509-0728
    (Lingerie & loungewear)

19. CARES
       COSMETICS, INC.
    1110 Oakwood Drive,
       SW
    Roanoke, VA 24015
       703-344-4280
    (Cosmetics—skin care
       & glamour)

20. CHAMBRÉ COSMETICS
       CORPORATION
    P.O. Box 6016
    Camarillo, CA 93010
       805-388-0735
    (Cosmetics & food
       supplements)

21. CHLON
       INTERNATIONAL, INC.
    19512 Livernois Avenue
    Detroit, MI 48221
       313-862-5851
    (Perfume)

22. COMPUCLUB
    MARKETING
    GROUP, INC.
    4901 Morena Boulevard
    Suite 402
    San Diego, CA 92117
      619-483-6100
    (Computer—home/hard
      & software)

23. CONCEPT NEW
    COSMETICS
    14000 Anson Street
    Santa Fe Springs, CA
    90670
      213-921-0534
    (Cosmetics)

24. CONSUMER
    EXPRESS, INC.
    202 West McNesse
    Street
    Lake Charles, LA 70605
      318-474-0505
    (Cosmetics/household &
      health food products)

25. THE CREATIVE CIRCLE
    15777 South Broadway
    Gardena, CA 90248
      213-327-1931
    (Craft/needlecraft kits)

26. CREATIVE
    EXPRESSIONS
    Rt. 422 West at Freeman
    P.O. Box 100
    Robesonia, PA 19551

      215-693-3191
    (Craft—stitchery/yarn)

27. DEBBIE HOWELL
    COSMETICS
    8650 South Lafayette
    Chicago, IL 68620
      312-874-5504
    (Cosmetics)

28. DECORA
    981 North Industrial
      Park Drive
    Orem, UT 84057
      801-225-1181
    (Decorative accessories)

29. DIAMITE CORPORATION
    131-D Albright Way
    Los Gatos, CA 95030
      408-866-7100
    (Jewelry/fashion)

30. DISCOVERY TOYS, INC.
    400 Ellinwood Way
    Suite 300
    Pleasant Hill, CA 94523
      415-680-8697
    (Toys—educational/books
      & games)

31. DONCASTER
    Box 1159
    Rutherfordton, NC 28139
      704-287-4205
    (Clothing—ladies dresses/
      coats/outerwear/
      sportswear)

32. DUDLEY PRODUCTS
    COMPANY
    3704 Old Battleground
    Road
    Greensboro, NC 27410
    919-282-0570
    (Cosmetics)

33. ELECTROLUX
    CORPORATION
    3003 Summer Street
    Stamford, CT 06905
    203-359-3600
    (Vacuum cleaners/
    floor polishers
    & attachments)

34. EMMA FAGE
    JEWELRY, LTD.
    P.O. Box 9724
    Austin, TX 78757
    512-452-0208
    (Jewelry)

35. EMMELINE COSMETICS
    CORPORATION
    3939 Washington Avenue
    Kansas City, MO 64111
    816-561-2400
    (Cosmetics)

36. ENCYCLOPAEDIA
    BRITANNICA, INC.
    Britannica Centre
    310 South Michigan
    Avenue
    Chicago, IL 60604
    312-347-7000

(Educational
publications/films)

37. EXCLUSIVELY BETTIE
    11842 Hamden Place
    Sante Fe Springs, CA
    90670
    213-949-8466
    (Clothing—lingerie &
    loungewear)

38. FASHION DYNAMICS
    1155 Triton Drive
    Suite D
    Foster City, CA 94404
    415-571-7766
    (Body & health care)

39. FASHION TWO
    TWENTY, INC.
    1263 South Chillicothe
    Road
    Aurora, OH 44202
    216-562-5111
    (Cosmetics)

40. FORTUNATE
    CORPORATION
    P.O. Box 5604
    Charlottesville, VA 22905
    804-977-5720
    (Pet/personal care/
    vitamins/home
    cleaning products)

41. FREEDOM MARKETING
    CORP.
    825 North Cass Avenue

Suite 311
Westmont, IL 60559
312-325-9009
(Food supplements/
weight-loss products)

42. THE FULLER BRUSH
COMPANY
2800 Rock Creek
Parkway
Suite 400
North Kansas City, MO
64117
816-474-1754
(Household cleaners/
industrial cleaning
products)

43. GOLDEN PRIDE, INC.
2628 Park Street
Lake Worth, FL 33460
305-586-7778
(Health & beauty aids)

44. GREAT AMERICAN
HEALTH &
NUTRITION, INC.
P.O. Box 6710
Fullerton, CA 92631
714-441-0788
(Food supplements)

45. GROLIER
INCORPORATED
Sherman Turnpike
Danbury, CT 06816
203-797-3500

(Educational
publications)

46. THE HANOVER
SHOE, INC.
118 Carlisle Street
Hanover, PA 17331
717-637-6631
(Shoes—men's
& women's)

47. HEALTH-MOR, INC.
151 East 22 Street
Lombard, IL 60148
312-953-9770
(Vacuum cleaners/Filter
Queen)

48. HIGHLIGHTS FOR
CHILDREN, INC.
2300 West Fifth Avenue
P.O. Box 269
Columbus, OH 43216
614-486-0631
(Educational
publications/
magazines)

49. HOME INTERIORS
& GIFTS, INC.
4550 Spring Valley Road
Dallas, TX 75234
214-386-1000
(Decorative accessories)

50. HOSTESS CHOICE
3201 E. Pioneer Parkway

#19–21, P.O. Box
121284
Arlington, TX 76012
817-649-2505
(Decorative accessories/
cleaners/food
seasoners)

51. HOUSE OF LLOYD, INC.
11901 Grandview Road
Grandview, MO 64030
816-763-7272
(Toys/jewelry/Christmas
decorations)

52. IDEAL PRODUCTS, INC.
1010 SE Everett Mall
Way
Suite 229
Everett, Wa 98204
206-347-4744
(Weight control/food
supplements)

53. JAFRA COSMETICS, INC.
P.O. Box 5026
Westlake Village, CA
91361
805-496-1911
(Cosmetics—skin care)

54. KAL-SON HOUSE, INC.
Shelard Plaza South,
#222
400 South Country
Road 18
Minneapolis, MN 55426
612-546-0303

(Food—Beef/gourmet—
flash frozen)

55. THE KIRBY COMPANY
1920 West 114 Street
Cleveland, OH
44102–2391
216-228-2400
(Vacuum cleaners)

56. KITCHEN FAIR
1090 Redmond Road
P.O. Box 100
Jacksonville, AR 72076
501-982-7446
(Cookware/stemware/
brass/kitchen gadgets)

57. LADY FINELLE
COSMETICS
137 Marston Street
P.O. Box 5200
Lawrence, MA
01842–2808
617-682-6112
(Cosmetics & skin care)

58. LADY LOVE
COSMETICS, INC.
2001 Walnut Hill Lane
P.O. Box 152015
Irving, TX 75061
214-255-5444
(Cosmetics & skin care
products)

59. LAURA LYNN
COSMETICS, INC.

5456 McConnell Avenue
Suite 189
Los Angeles, CA 90066
  213-306-4540
(Cosmetics/skin care/
  color by season
  consultation)

60. LEARNER'S WORLD
  6151 West Century
    Boulevard
  Suite 400
  Los Angeles, CA 90045
    213-641-9645
  (Toys)

61. LEARNEX LTD., INC.
  89 Saw Mill River Road
  Elmsford, NY 10523
    914-592-1770
  (Publications—children's
    cassettes/books/
    educational toys)

62. LEGACY
    INTERNATIONAL, INC.
  4211 North Main Street
  P.O. Box 5648
  High Point, NC 27262
    919-869-1101
  (Household/nutritional
    care/jewelry &
    automotive)

63. LUCKY HEART
    COSMETICS, INC.
  138 Huling Avenue
  Memphis, TN 38103

  901-526-7658
  (Cosmetics & jewelry)

64. LYNELL'S SKIN
    CARE, LTD.
  1153 Chess Drive
  Foster City, CA 94404
    415-571-1282
  (Cosmetics & skin care)

65. MAGIK MAID
  P.O. Box 1611
  Flint, MI 48501
    313-239-7677
  (Personal care products)

66. MARLOW HALL, INC.
  3914 Sandshell
  Ft. Worth, TX 76137
    817-232-9612
  (Cosmetics)

67. MARY CATHERINE, INC.
  601 East Biddison
  Box 11401
  Fort Worth, TX 76109
    817-927-8408
  (Clothing/semiprecious
    jewelry)

68. MARY KAY
    COSMETICS, INC.
  8787 Stemmons Freeway
  Dallas, TX 75247
    214-630-8787
  (Cosmetics)

69. MASON SHOE
      MANUFACTURING
      COMPANY
    1251 First Avenue
    Chippewa Falls, WI
      54729
      715-723-1871
    (Shoes—men's
      & women's)

70. McCONNON &
      COMPANY
    McConnon Drive
    Winona, MN 55987
      507-452-2910
    (Household products/
      animal care products/
      health care
      products/insecticides)

71. MIRACLE MAID
    P.O. Box C-50
    Redmond, WA 98052
      206-881-6171
    (Cookware)

72. NATURAL IMPRESSIONS
      CORPORATION
    182 Liberty Street
    Painesville, OH 44077
      216-357-8950
    (Jewelry)

73. NEO-LIFE COMPANY
      OF AMERICA
    25000 Industrial
      Boulevard
    P.O. Box 5015

Hayward, CA 94540
  415-786-3401
(Household products/
  vitamins/minerals/
  food/water)

74. NOEVIR, INC.
    1095 SE Main Street
    Irvine, CA 92714
      714-660-1111
    (Cosmetics)

75. NUTRI-METICS
      INTERNATIONAL, INC.
    19501 East Walnut Drive
    City of Industry, CA
      91749
      714-598-1831
    (Cosmetics/food
      supplements/bras)

76. ORIFLAME
      CORPORATION
    76 Treble Cove Road
    North Billerica, MA
      08162
      617-663-2700
    (Cosmetics—European
      skin care)

77. PARTYLITE GIFTS
    Building 16
    Cordage Park
    Plymouth, MA 02360
      617-775-2500
    (Decorative accessories/
      giftware)

78. PERFUME
    ORIGINALS, INC.
    45 West 34 Street
    New York, NY 10001
    212-695-9494
    (Perfume)

79. PERSONAL RESOURCE
    SYSTEM, INC.
    1307 Stratford Court
    P.O. Box 2529
    Del Mar, CA 92014
    619-755-5664
    (Personal organization/
    time-management
    system)

80. POLA U.S.A., INC.
    250 East Victoria Avenue
    Carson, CA 90746
    213-770-6000
    (Cosmetics)

81. PRINCESS HOUSE, INC.
    455 Somerset Avenue
    North Dighton, MA
    02764
    617-823-0713
    (Decorative accessories/
    crystal)

82. QUEEN'S-WAY TO
    FASHION, INC.
    2500 Crawford Avenue
    Evanston, IL 60201
    312-492-1400
    (Clothing—women's)

83. THE W. T. RAWLEIGH
    COMPANY
    223 East Main Street
    Freeport, IL 61032
    815-232-4161
    (Household products—
    foods/cleaning/
    medicine/pet)

84. REGAL WARE, INC.
    1675 Reigle Drive
    Kewaskum, WI 53040
    414-626-2121
    (Cookware)

85. RENA-WARE
    DISTRIBUTORS, INC.
    P.O. Box C-50
    Redmond, WA 98052
    206-881-6171
    (Cookware)

86. ROSE JOYCE
    COSMETICS
    CORPORATION
    13037 Dorothy Drive
    Philadelphia, PA 19116
    215-677-8770
    (Cosmetics)

87. ROYAL AMERICAN
    FOOD COMPANY
    24307 East 40 Highway
    P.O. Box 1000
    Blue Springs, MO 64015
    816-229-1000
    (Food—whey-based/
    dehydrated)

88. ROYAL DESIGNS, INC.
    1710 Firman Drive
    Suite 100
    Richardson, TX 75081
    214-480-0055
    (Jewelry)

89. SALADMASTER, INC.
    131 Howell Street
    Dallas, TX 75207
    214-742-2222
    (Cookware/tableware)

90. SASCO
    COSMETICS, INC.
    2151 Hutton Drive
    Carrollton, TX 75006
    214-484-3950
    (Cosmetics/personal
    care/primarily
    Aloe Vera)

91. SHAKLEE
    CORPORATION
    Shaklee Terraces
    444 Market Street
    San Francisco, CA 94111
    415-954-3000
    (Food supplements/
    foods/personal care
    products)

92. SHAREX
    P.O. Box 19649
    Irvine, CA 92713
    714-261-8700
    (Food—Country Spring, a
    dry milk replacer)

93. SILVAN EVE
    5600 Oakbrook Parkway
    Suite 170
    Norcross, GA 30093
    404-448-1222
    (Jewelry—silver/gold)

94. SOCIETY CORPORATION
    1609 Kilgore Avenue
    Muncie, IN 47304
    317-289-3318
    (Cookware, china,
    crystal)

95. THE SOUTHWESTERN
    COMPANY
    P.O. Box 820
    Nashville, TN 37202
    615-790-4000
    (Educational
    publications)

96. STANHOME, INC.
    333 Western Avenue
    Westfield, MA 01085
    413-562-3631
    (Household cleaning
    products & good
    grooming aids)

97. STEP's ADVENTURES
    WITH THE 3R's
    8521—44 Avenue West
    P.O. Box 887
    Mukilteo, WA 98275
    206-355-9830
    (Educational programs—

reading/math/
perceptual tasks)

98. STERLING HEALTH
    SERVICES
    CORPORATION
    3900 South Florida
    Avenue
    P.O. Box 6500
    Lakeland, FL 33807
    813-644-7581
    (Health appraisals—
    custom/food
    supplements)

99. THE STUART McGUIRE
    COMPANY, INC.
    115 Brand Road
    Salem, VA 24156
    703-389-8121
    (Shoes & clothing—men
    & women)

100. SYBIL'S
     9034 Natural Bridge
     Road
     St. Louis, MO 63121
     314-426-2100
     (Jewelry & fragrances)

101. TANDY HOME
     EDUCATION SYSTEMS
     1301 West 22 Street
     Suite 400
     Oak Brook, IL 60521
     312-325-6150
     (Home computer
     systems)

102. TCC
     INTERNATIONAL, LTD.
     Route 1, P.O. Box 130
     Cape Neddick, ME
     03902
     207-363-6695
     (Cosmetics—skin care
     products)

103. TIARA EXCLUSIVES
     717 East Street
     Dunkirk, IN 47336
     317-768-6789
     (Decorative accessories/
     glassware)

104. TIME-LIFE BOOKS, INC.
     777 Duke Street
     Alexandria, VA 22314
     703-838-7000
     (Educational
     publications)

105. TOMORROW'S
     TREASURES, INC.
     111 North Glassboro
     Road
     Woodbury Heights, NJ
     08097
     609-468-5656
     (Photo albums/
     photography/cameras)

106. TRI-CHEM, INC.
     One Cape May Street
     Harrison, NJ 07029
     201-482-5500

(Craft products—liquid
embroidery paint)

107. TUPPERWARE
P.O. Box 2353
Orlando, FL 32802
305-847-1871
(Household products)

108. U.S. SAFETY &
ENGINEERING
CORPORATION
2365 El Camino Avenue
Sacramento, CA 95821
916-482-8888
(Security systems—fire/
burglar)

109. UNITED CONSUMER
CLUB, INC.
8450 South Broadway
Merrillville, IN 46410
219-736-1100
(Buyers service)

110. UNITED LABORATORIES
OF AMERICA, INC.
1526 Fort Worth Avenue
P.O. Box 4499, Station A
Dallas, TX 75208
214-741-4461
(Photo albums/Bibles/
books/photo
enlargements)

111. VITA CRAFT
CORPORATION
11100 West 58 Street

P.O. Box 3129
Shawnee, KS 66203
913-631-6265
(Cookware/china/crystal/
tableware/cutlery)

112. VORWERK USA, INC.
500 Northlake Boulevard
South
Altamonte Springs, FL
32701
305-339-8321
(Housewares—carpet &
floor care equipment)

113. WATKINS
INCORPORATED
150 Liberty Street
Winona, MN 55987
507-457-3300
(Household—food/health/
cleaning products)

114. THE WEST BEND
COMPANY
400 Washington Street
West Bend, WI 53095
414-334-2311
(Cookware & electrical
appliances)

115. WORLD BOOK, INC.
510 Merchandise Mart
Plaza
Chicago, IL 60654
312-245-3456
(Educational
publications)